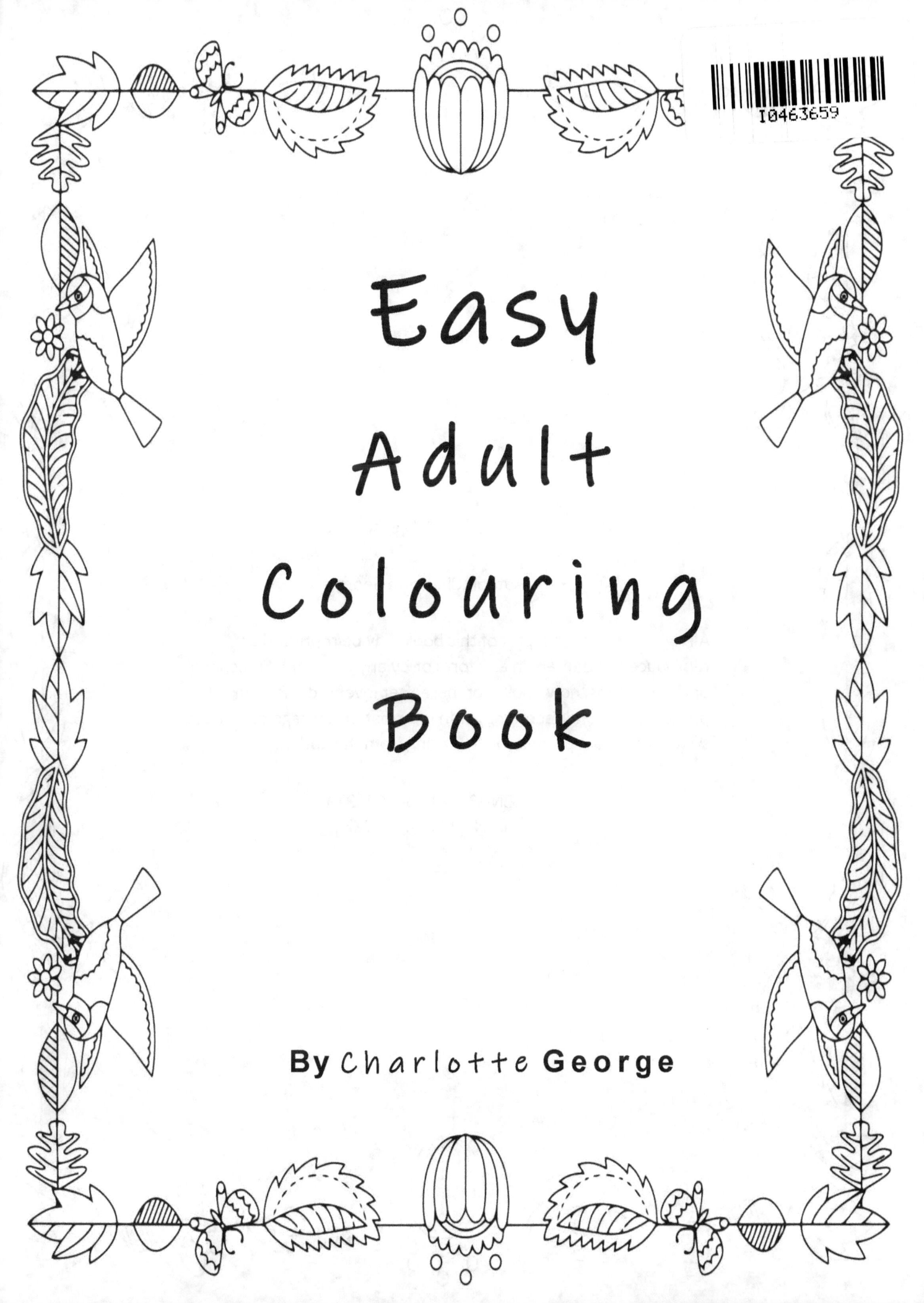

Easy Adult Colouring Book

By Charlotte George

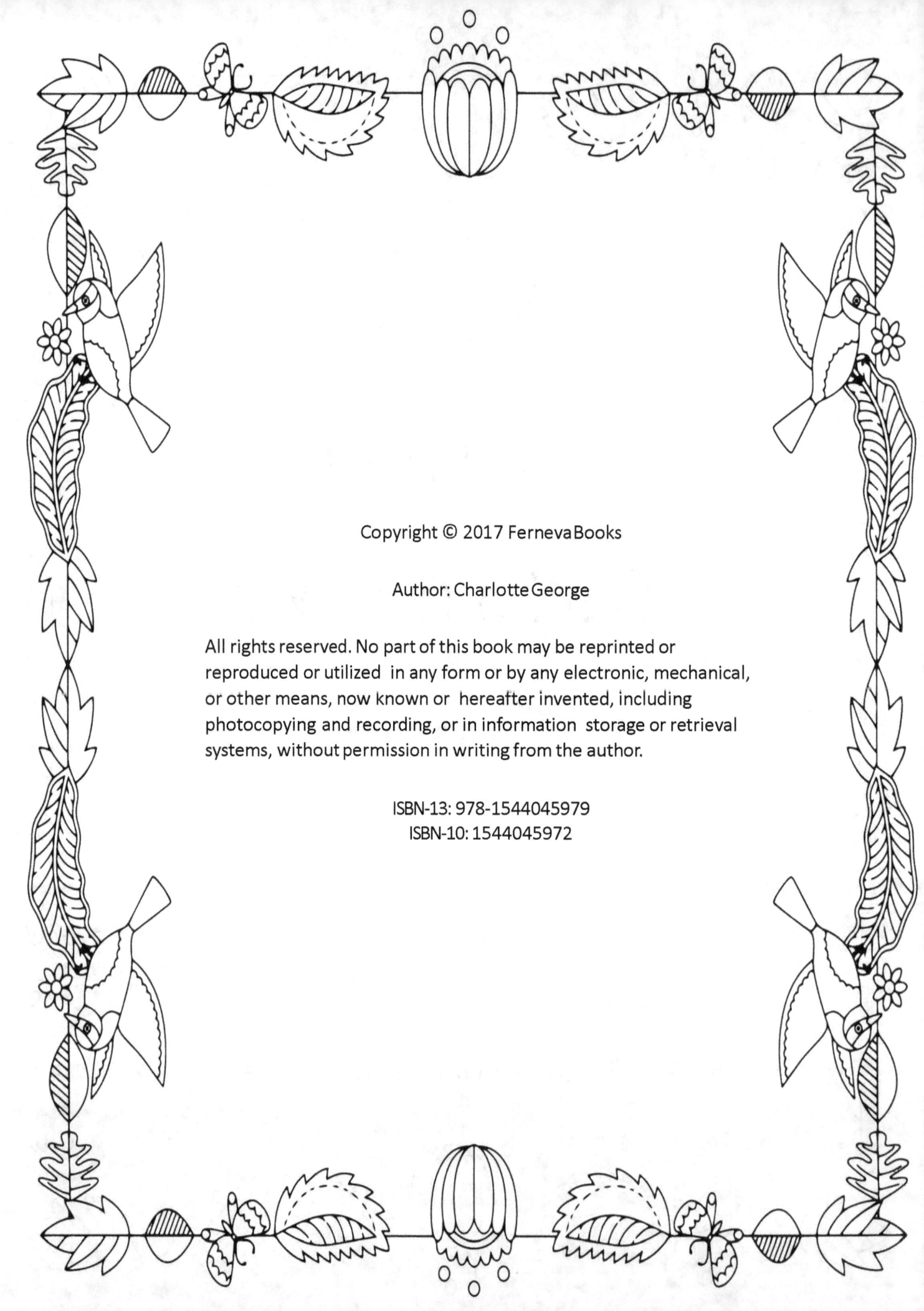

ISBN-13: 978-1544045979
ISBN-10: 1544045972

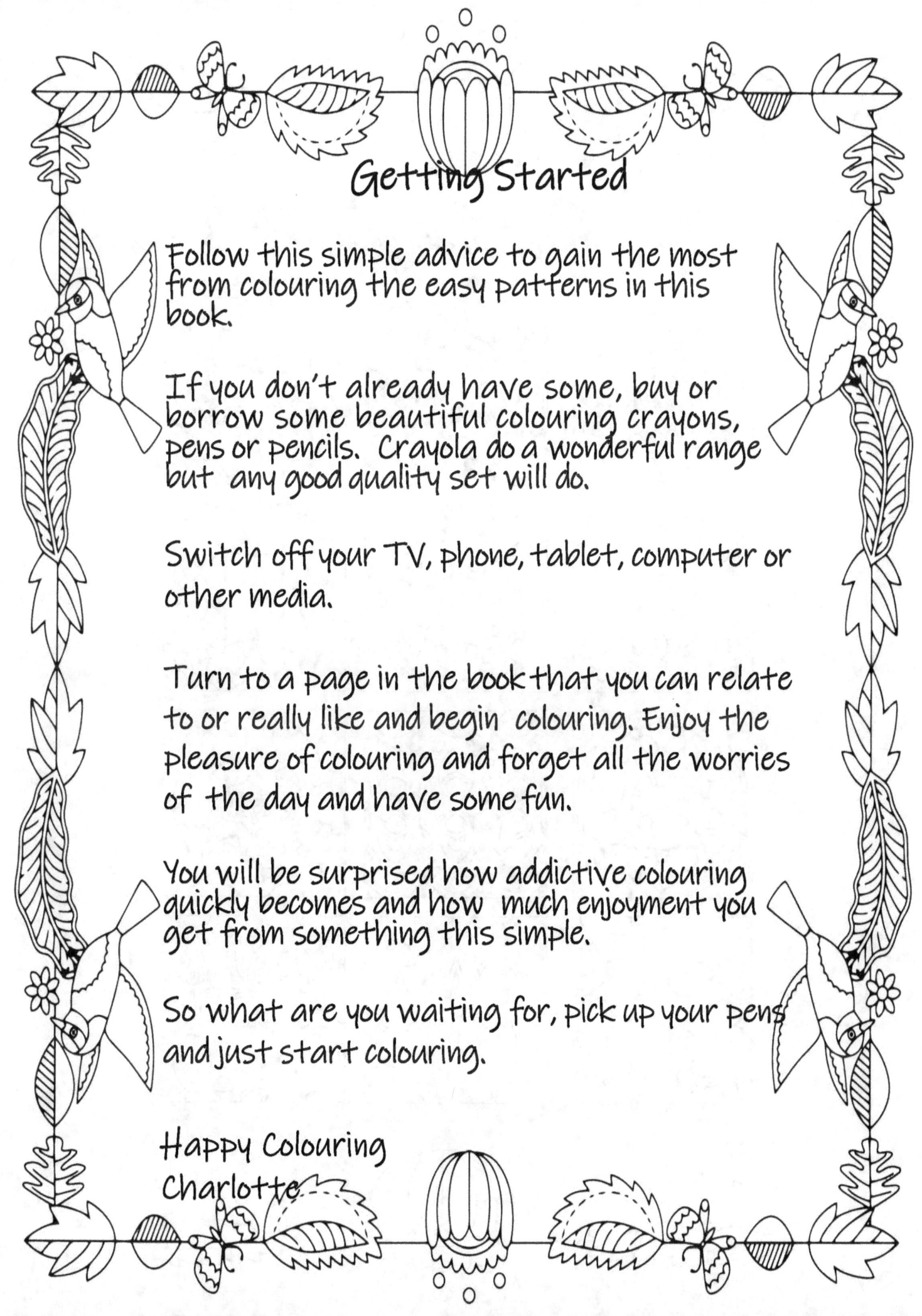

Getting Started

Follow this simple advice to gain the most from colouring the easy patterns in this book.

If you don't already have some, buy or borrow some beautiful colouring crayons, pens or pencils. Crayola do a wonderful range but any good quality set will do.

Switch off your TV, phone, tablet, computer or other media.

Turn to a page in the book that you can relate to or really like and begin colouring. Enjoy the pleasure of colouring and forget all the worries of the day and have some fun.

You will be surprised how addictive colouring quickly becomes and how much enjoyment you get from something this simple.

So what are you waiting for, pick up your pens and just start colouring.

Happy Colouring
Charlotte

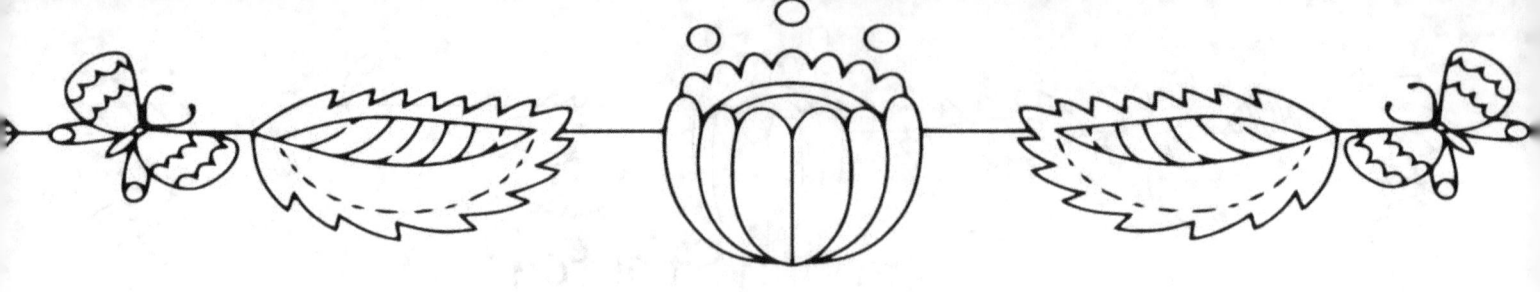

Samples in Book

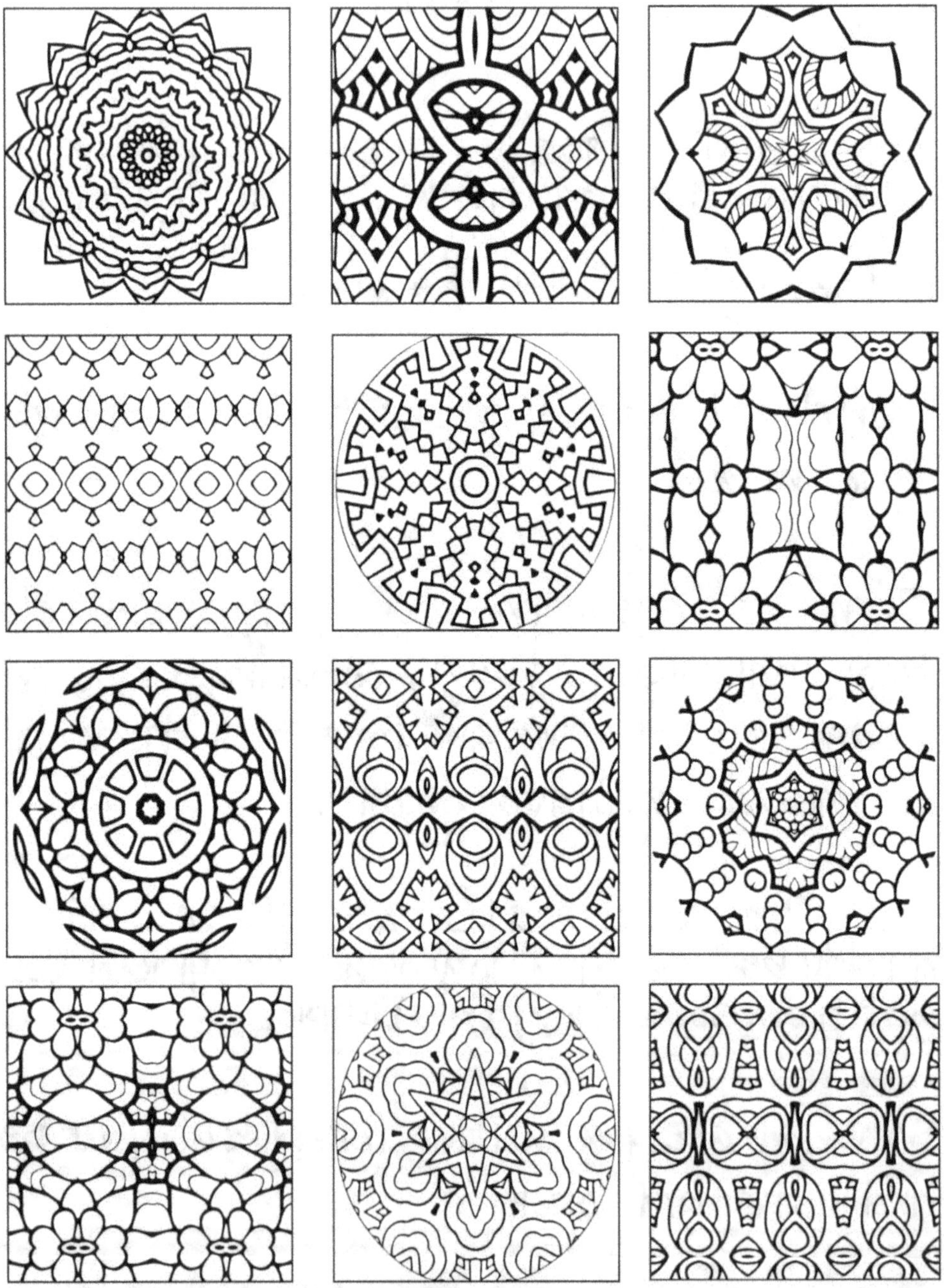

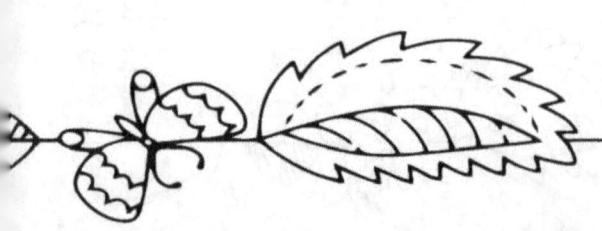
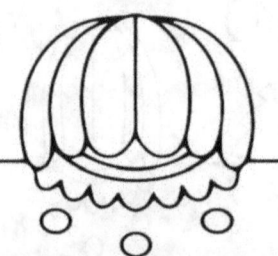
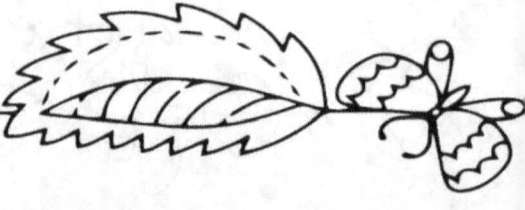

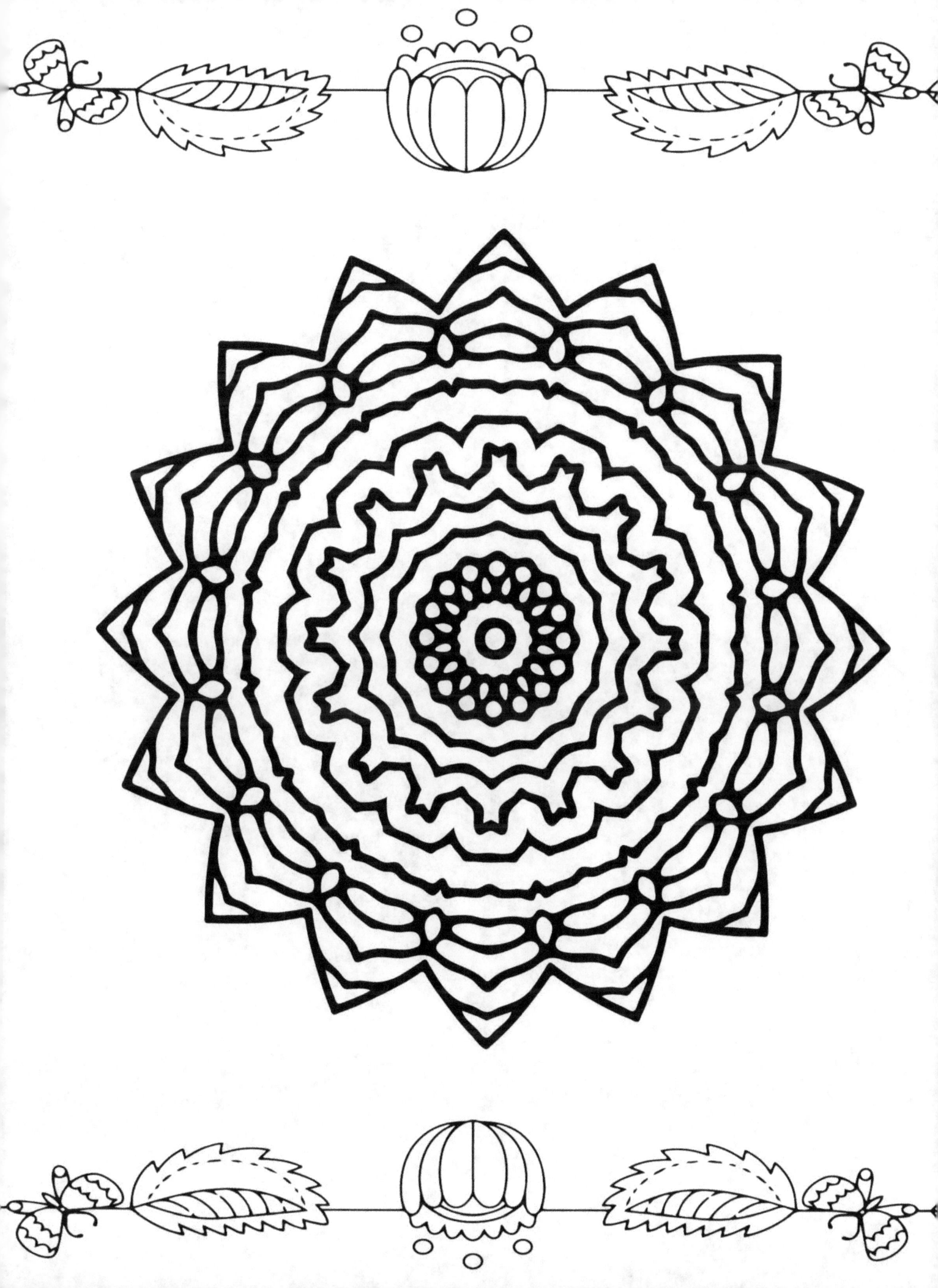

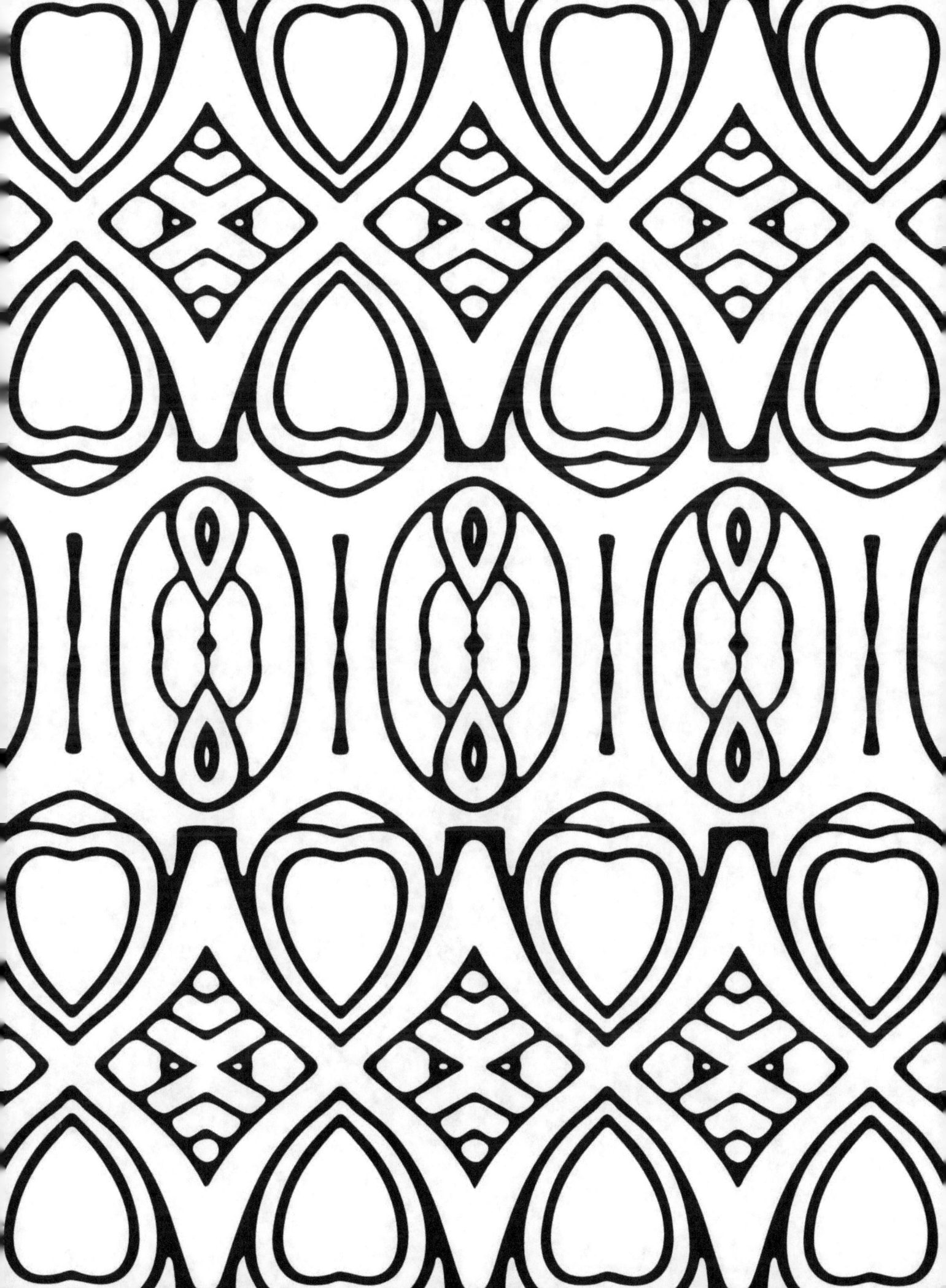

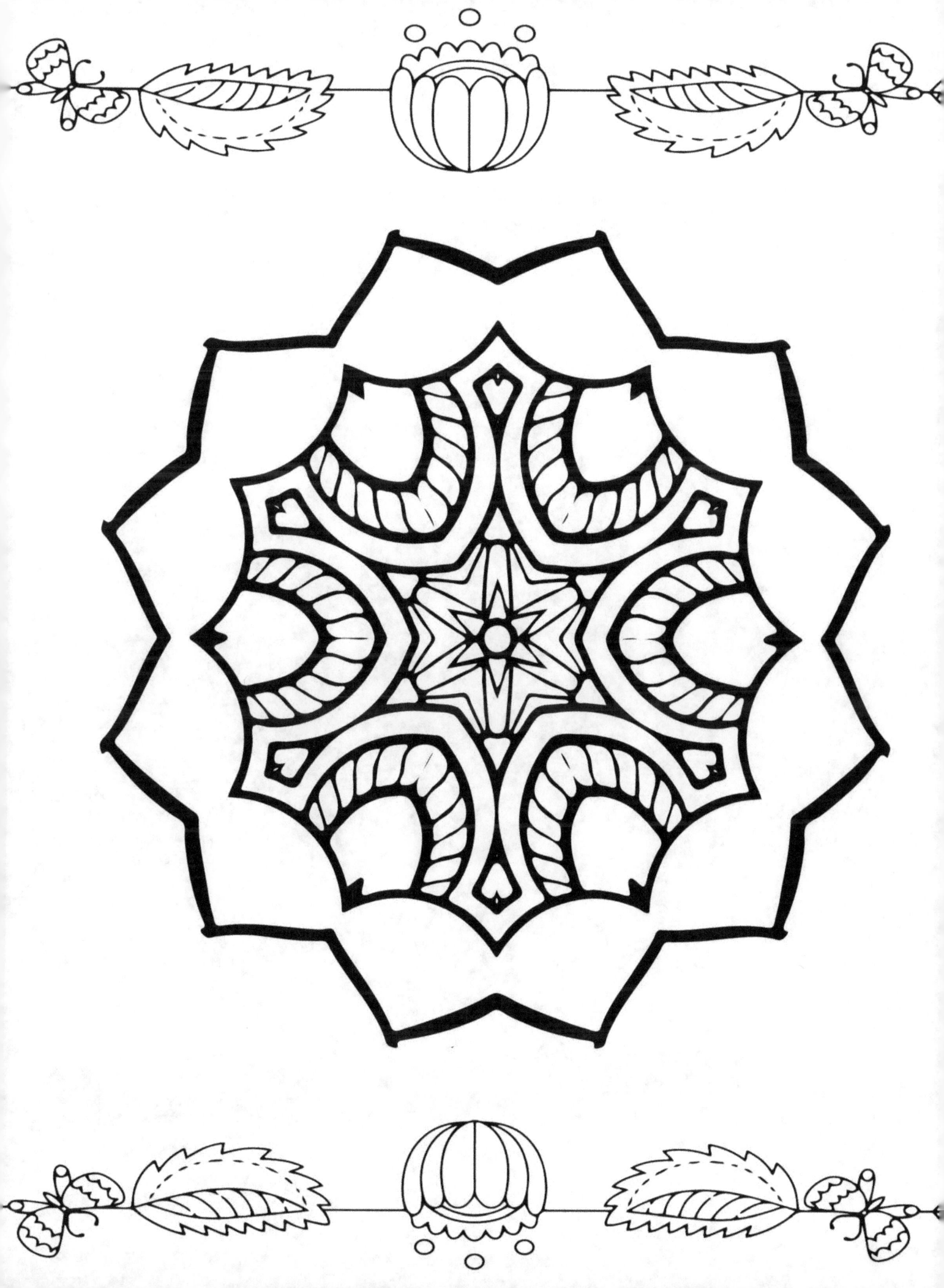

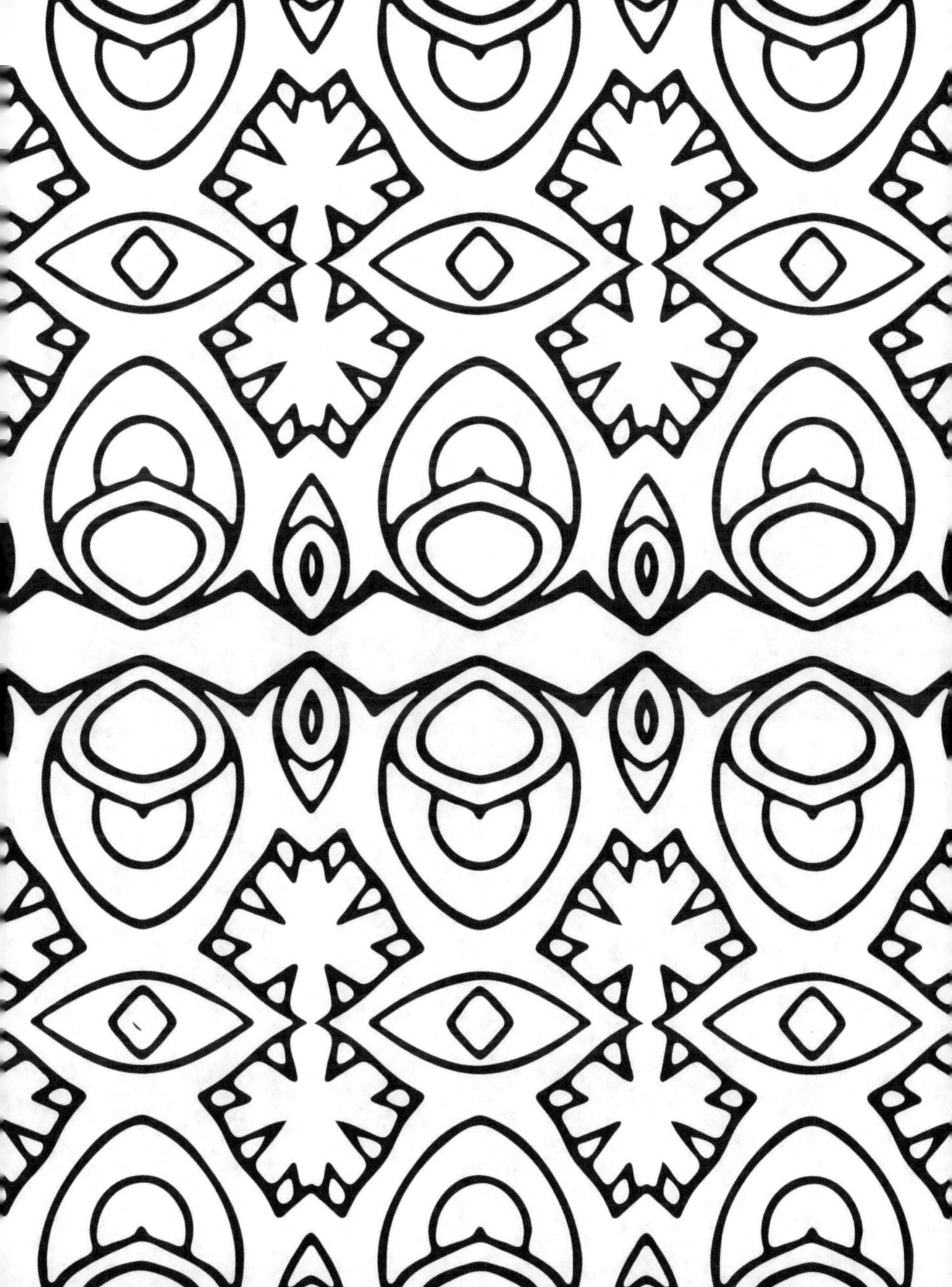

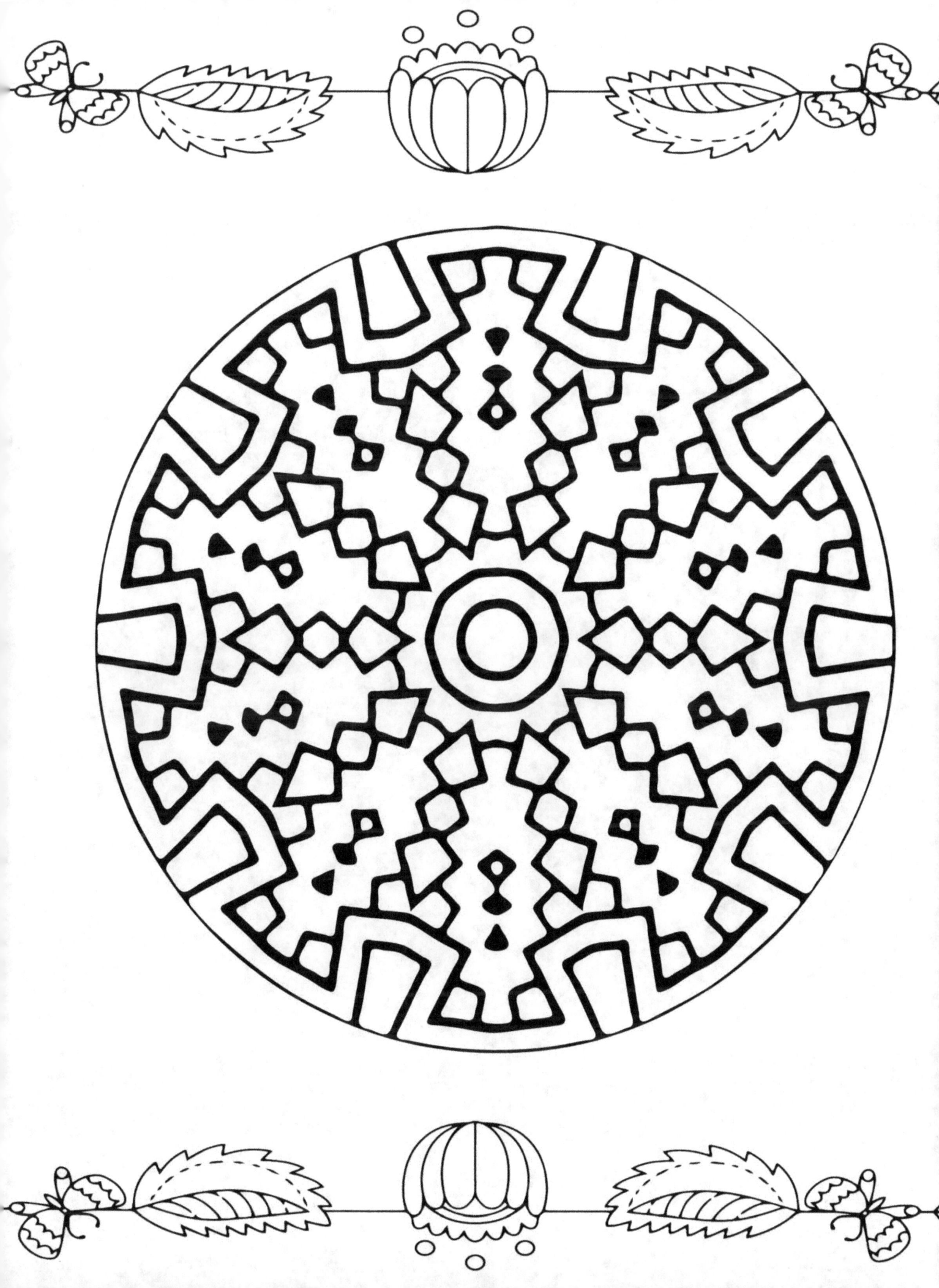

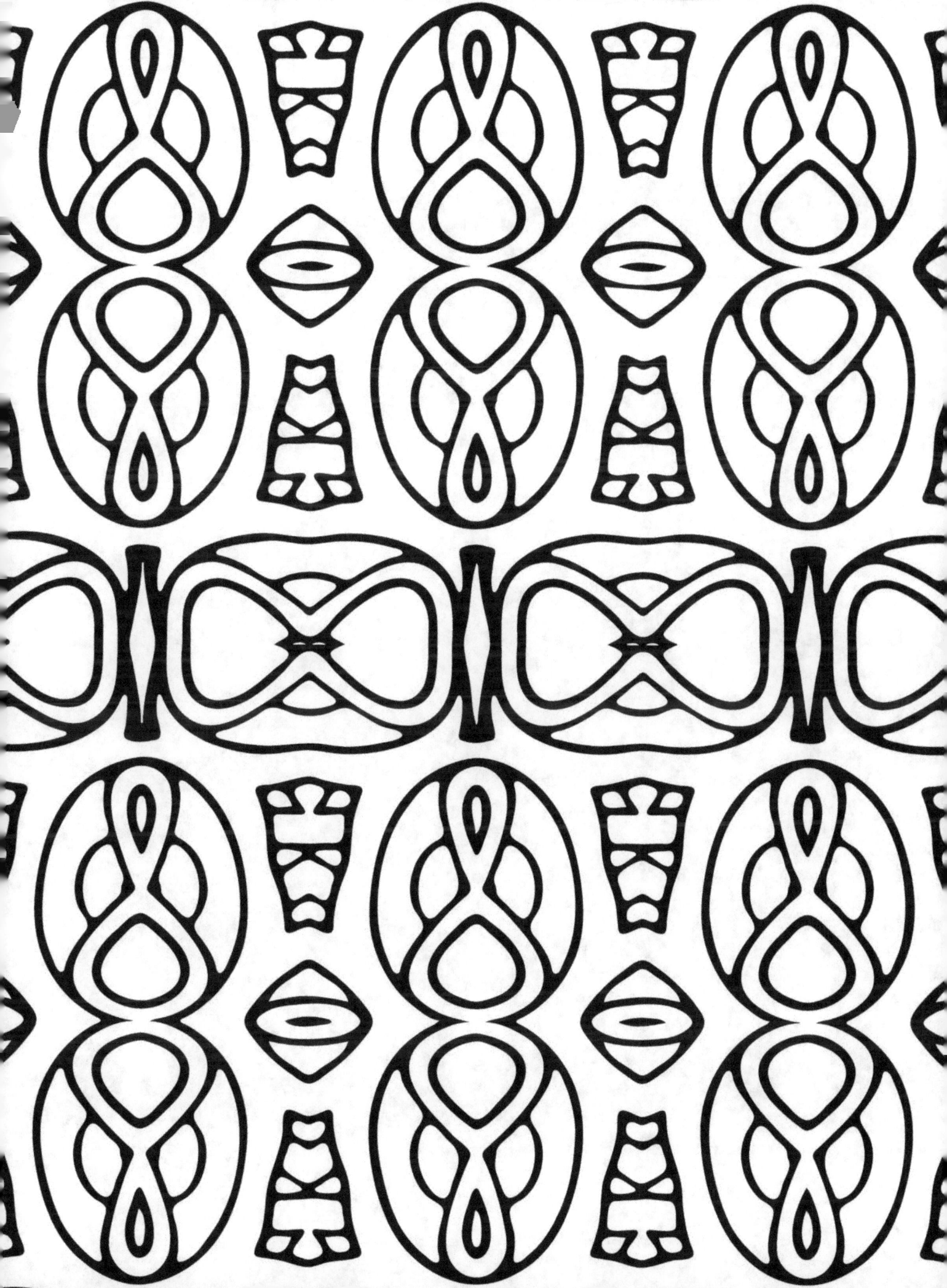

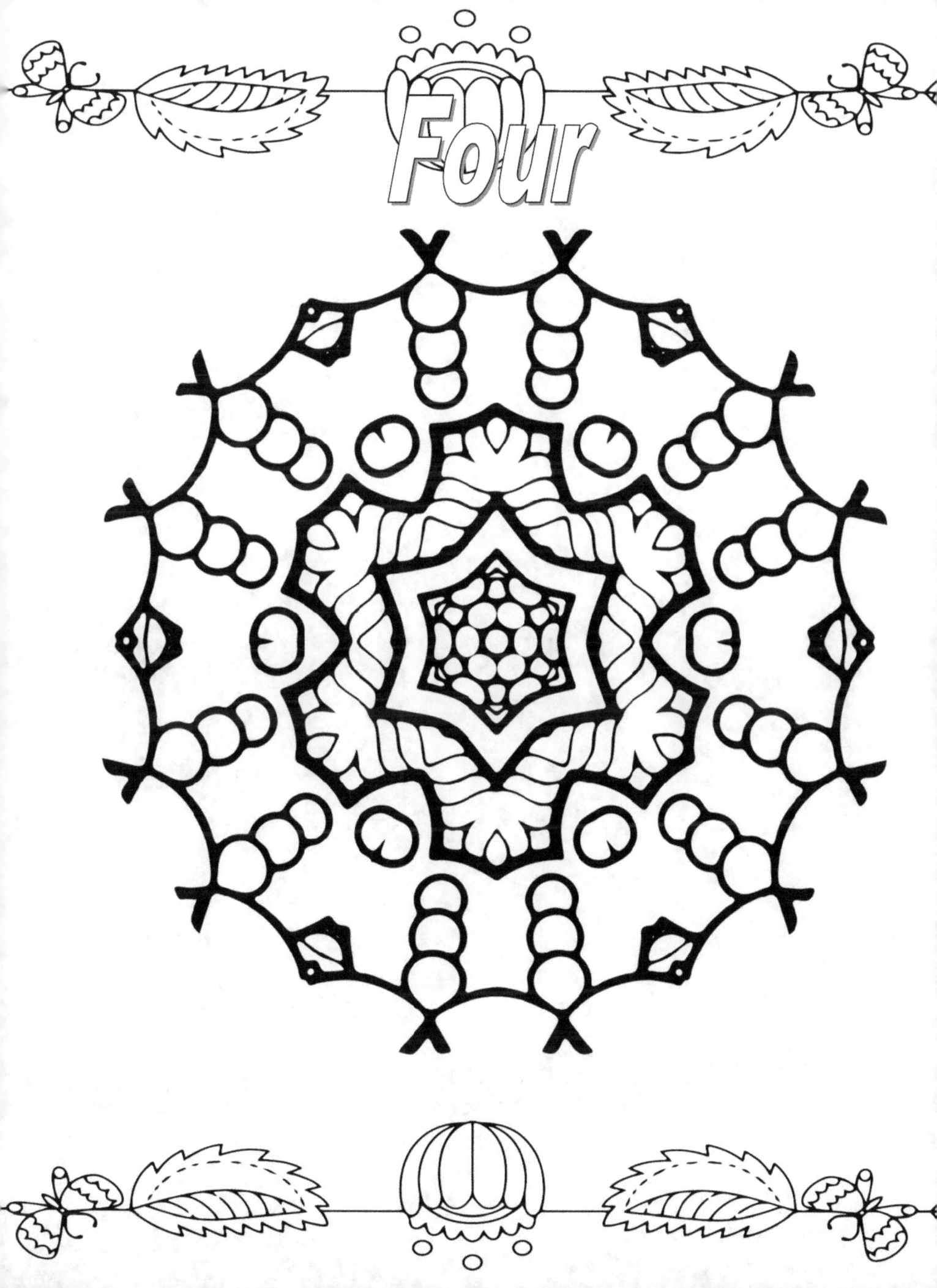

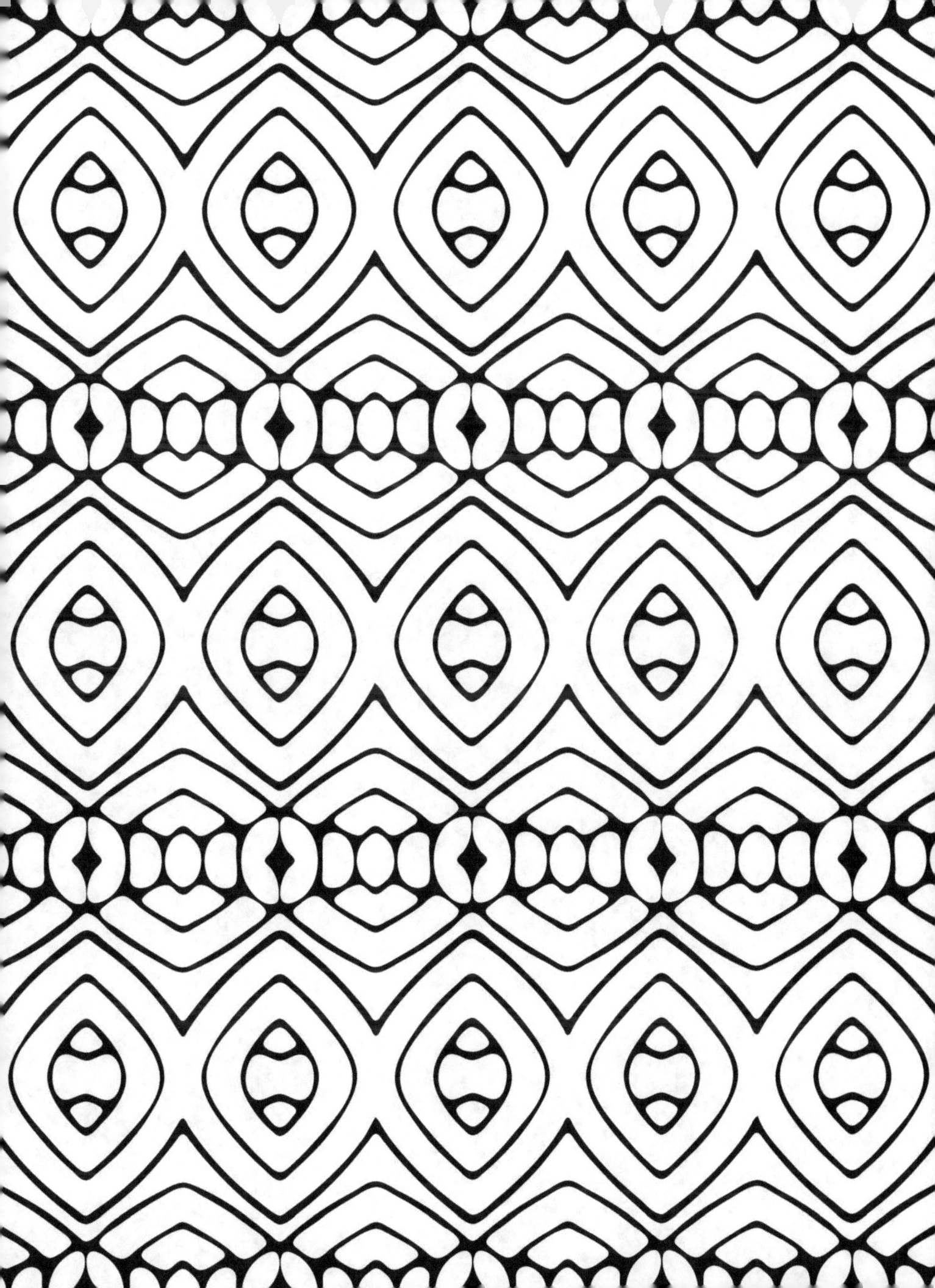

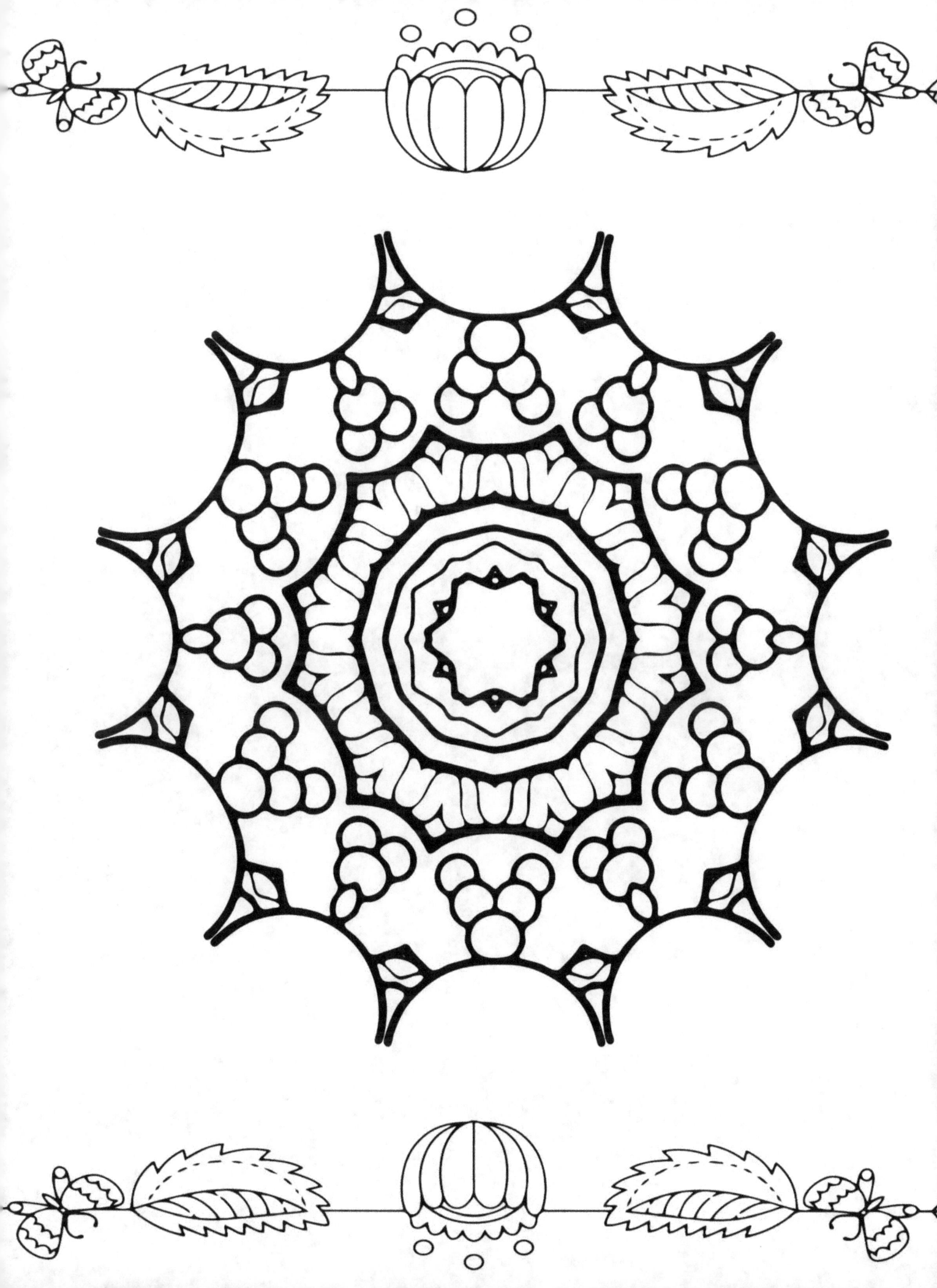

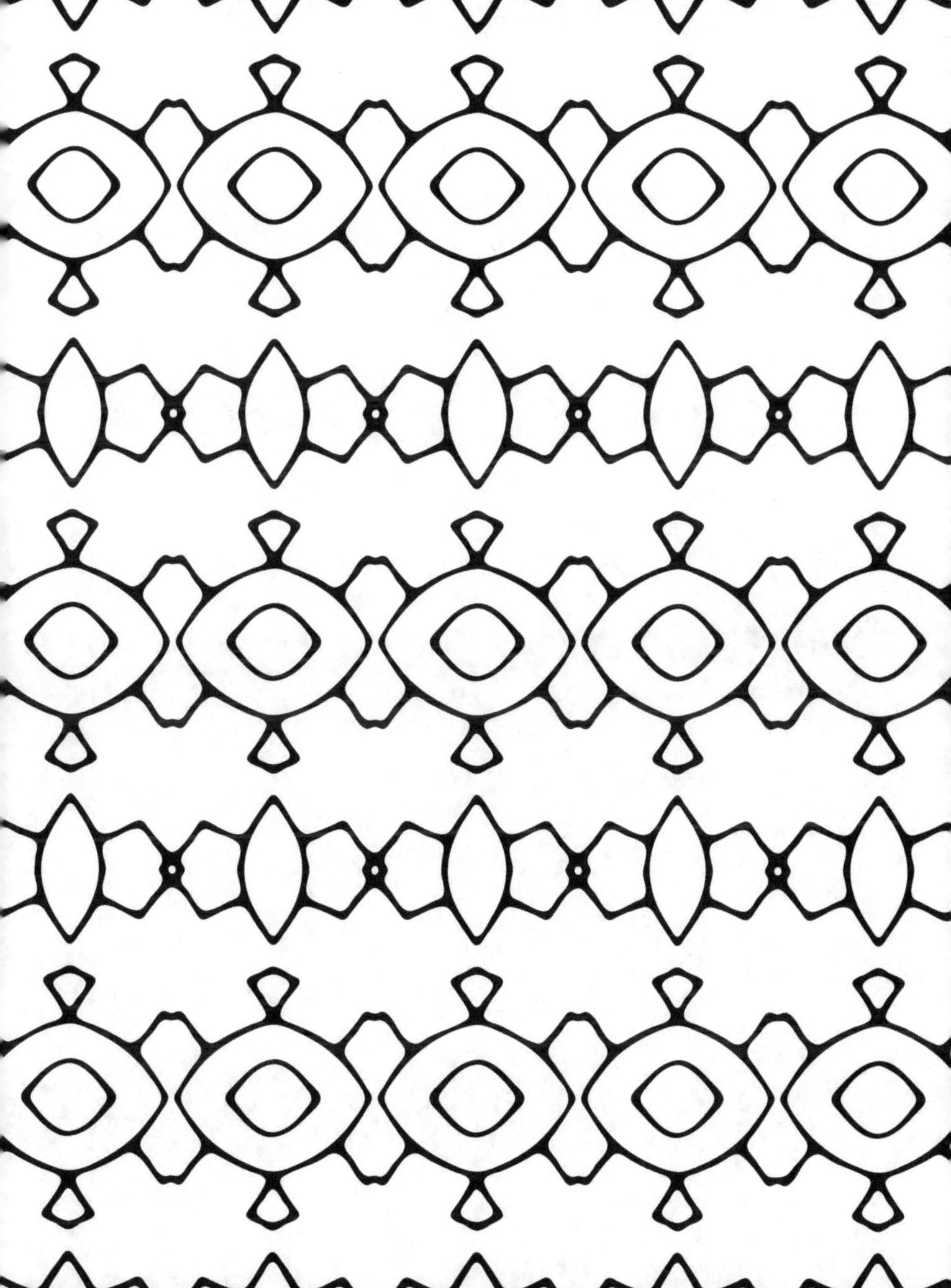

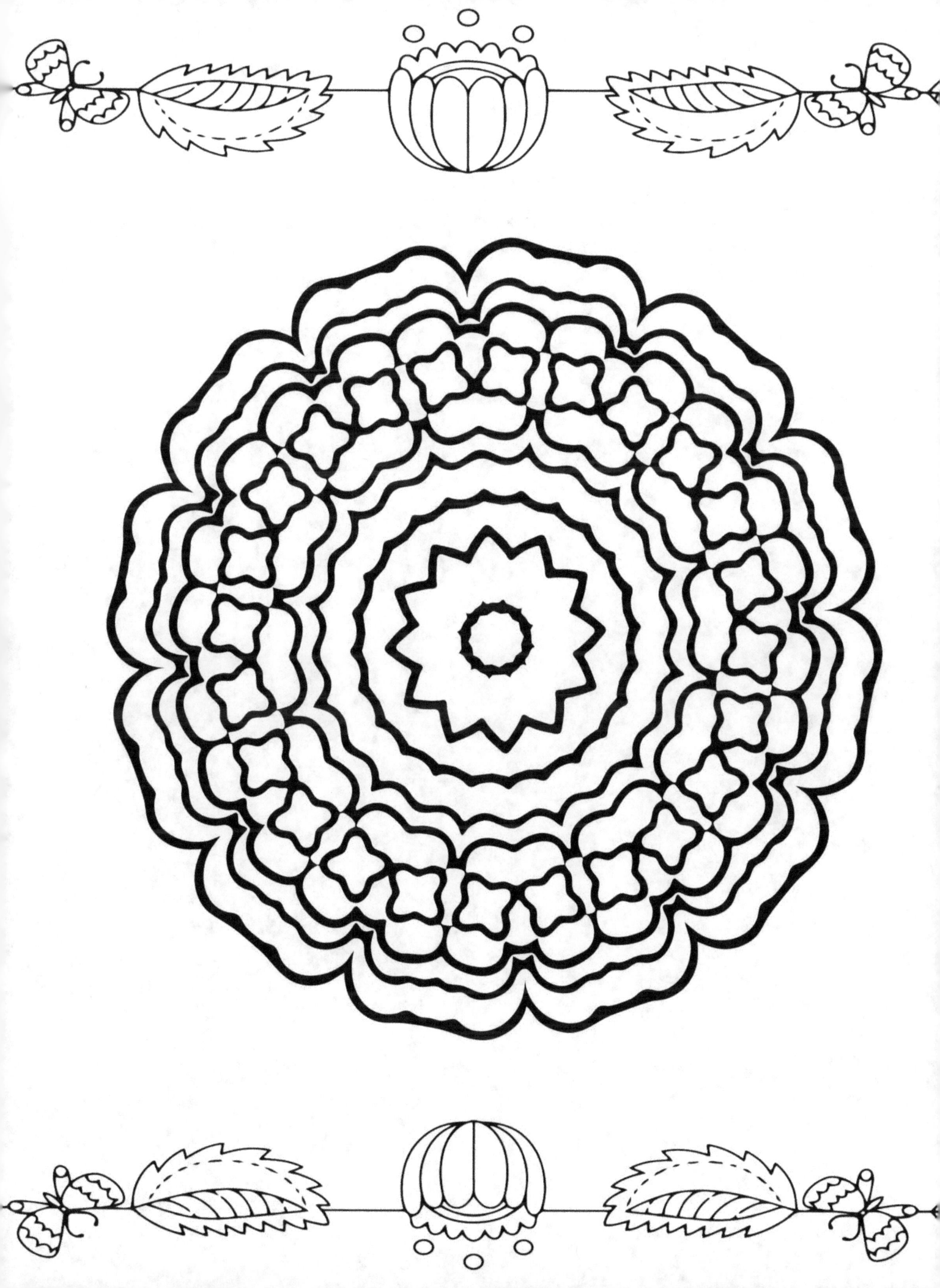

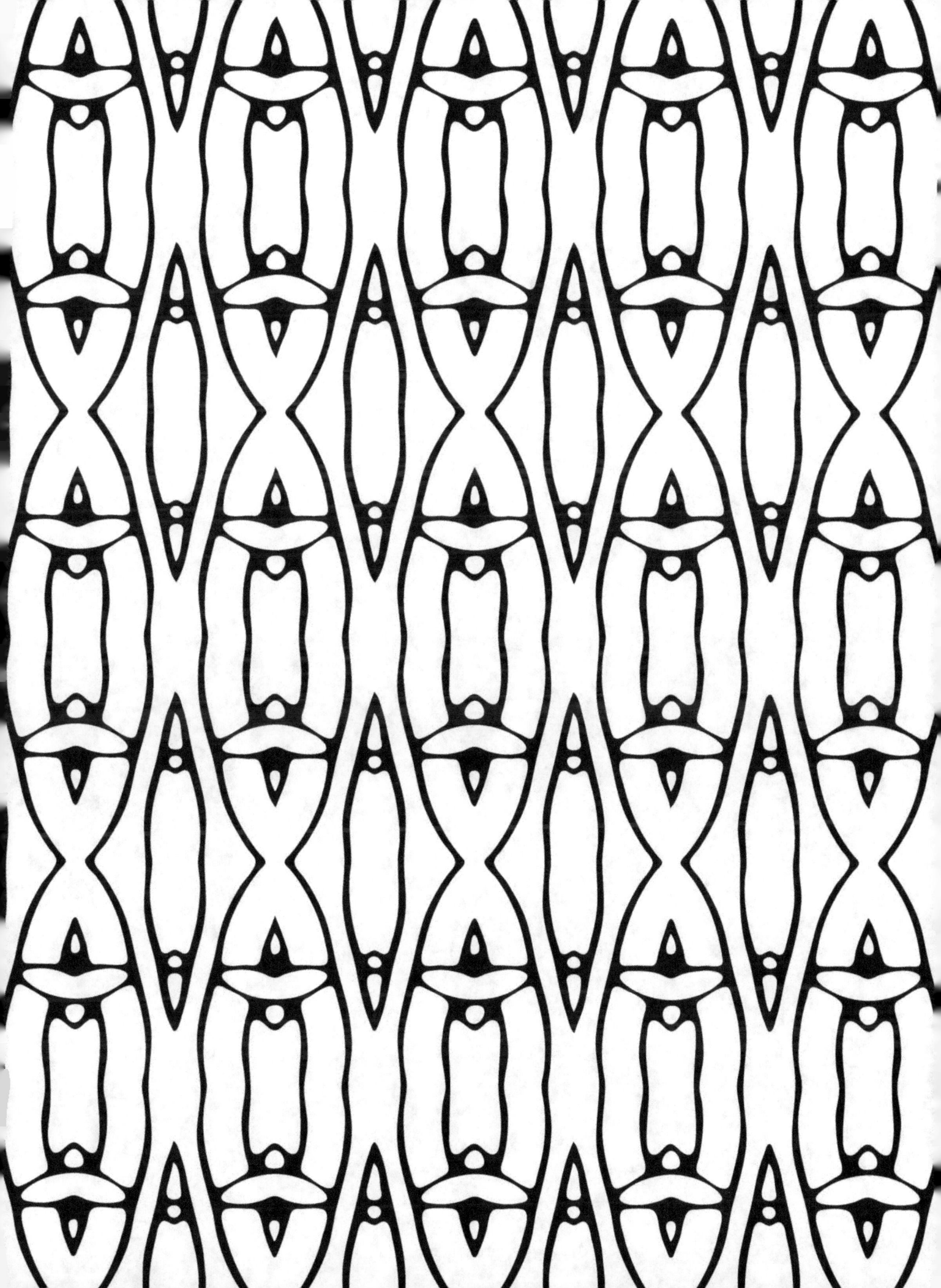

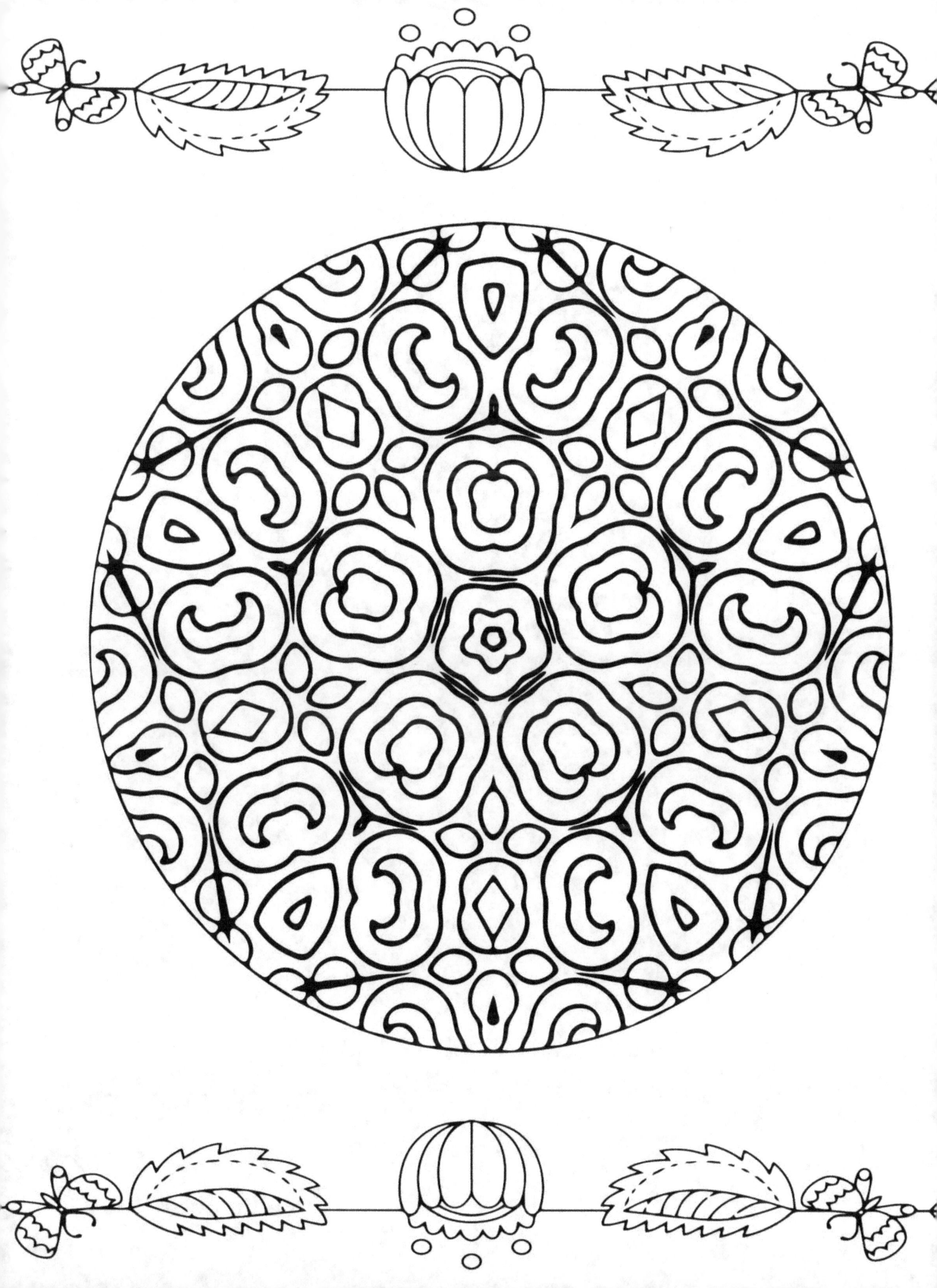

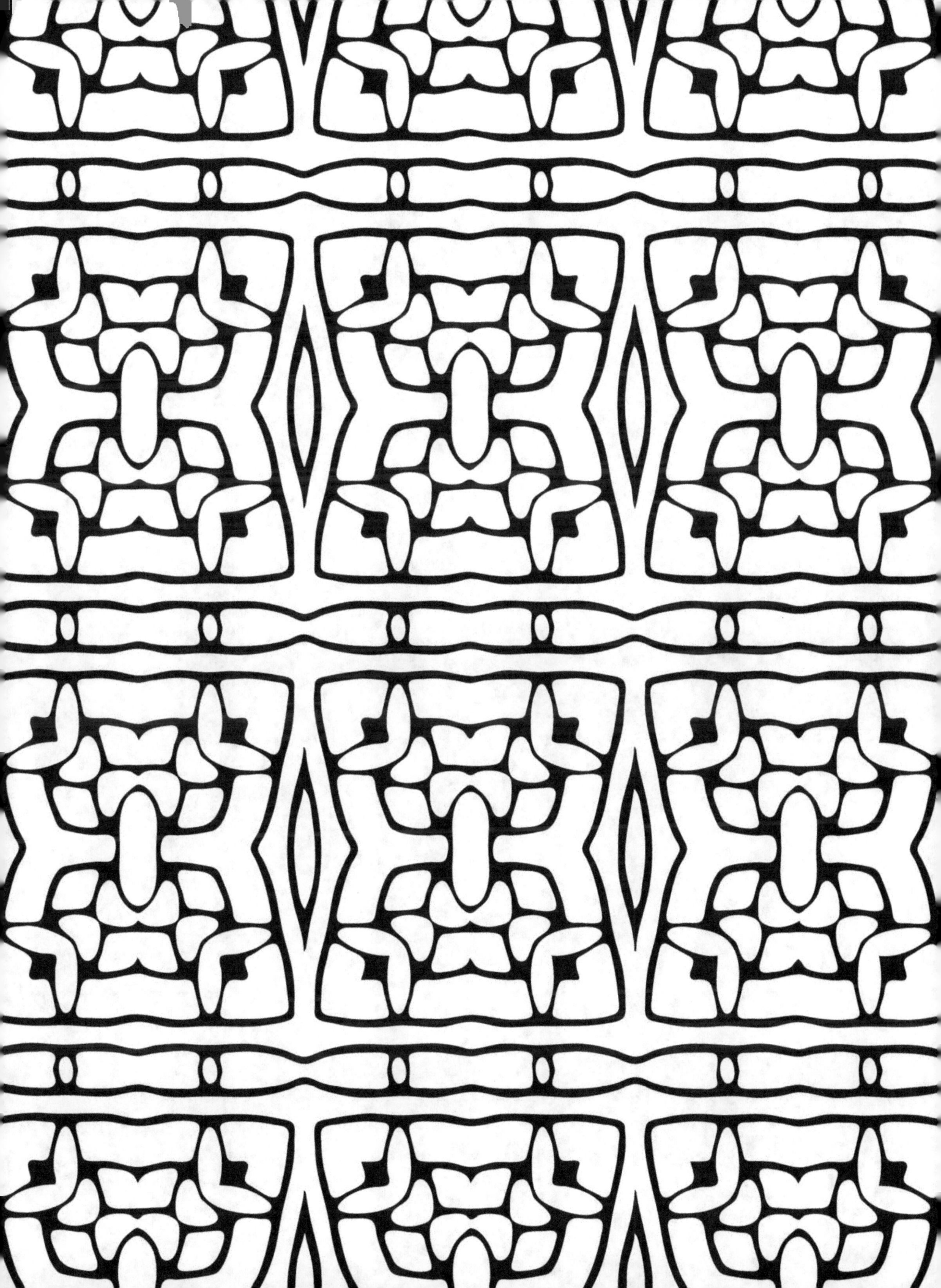

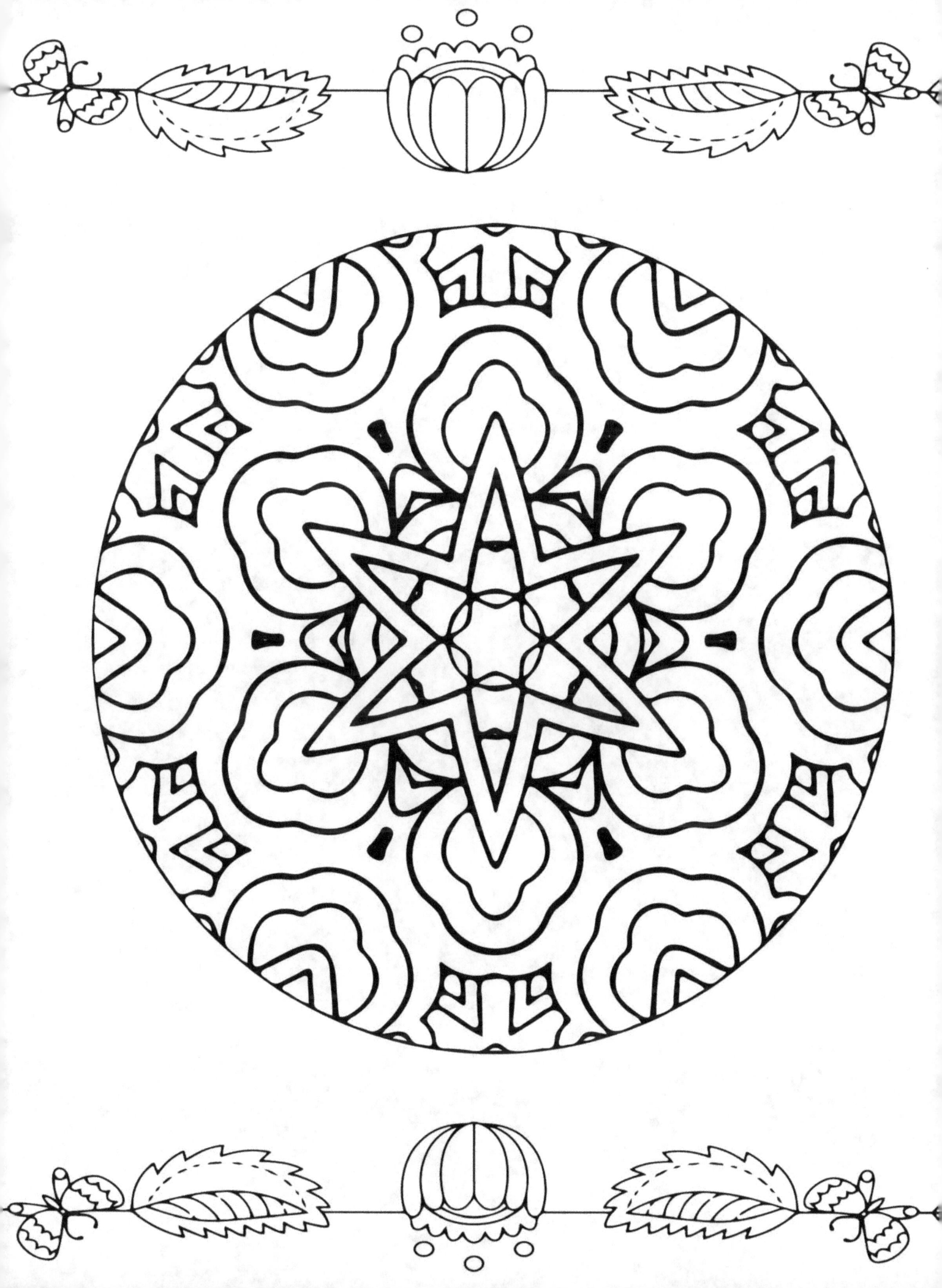

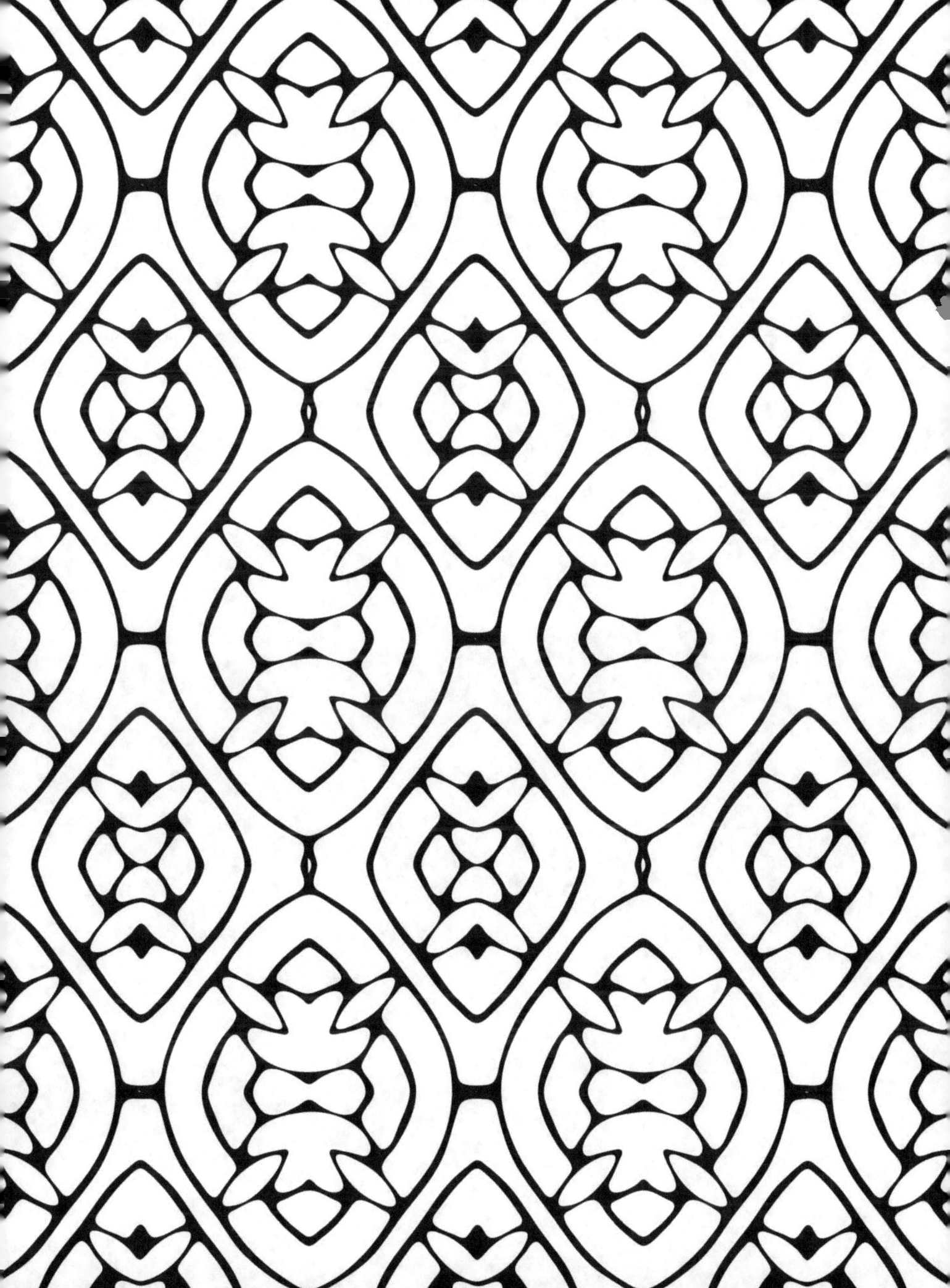

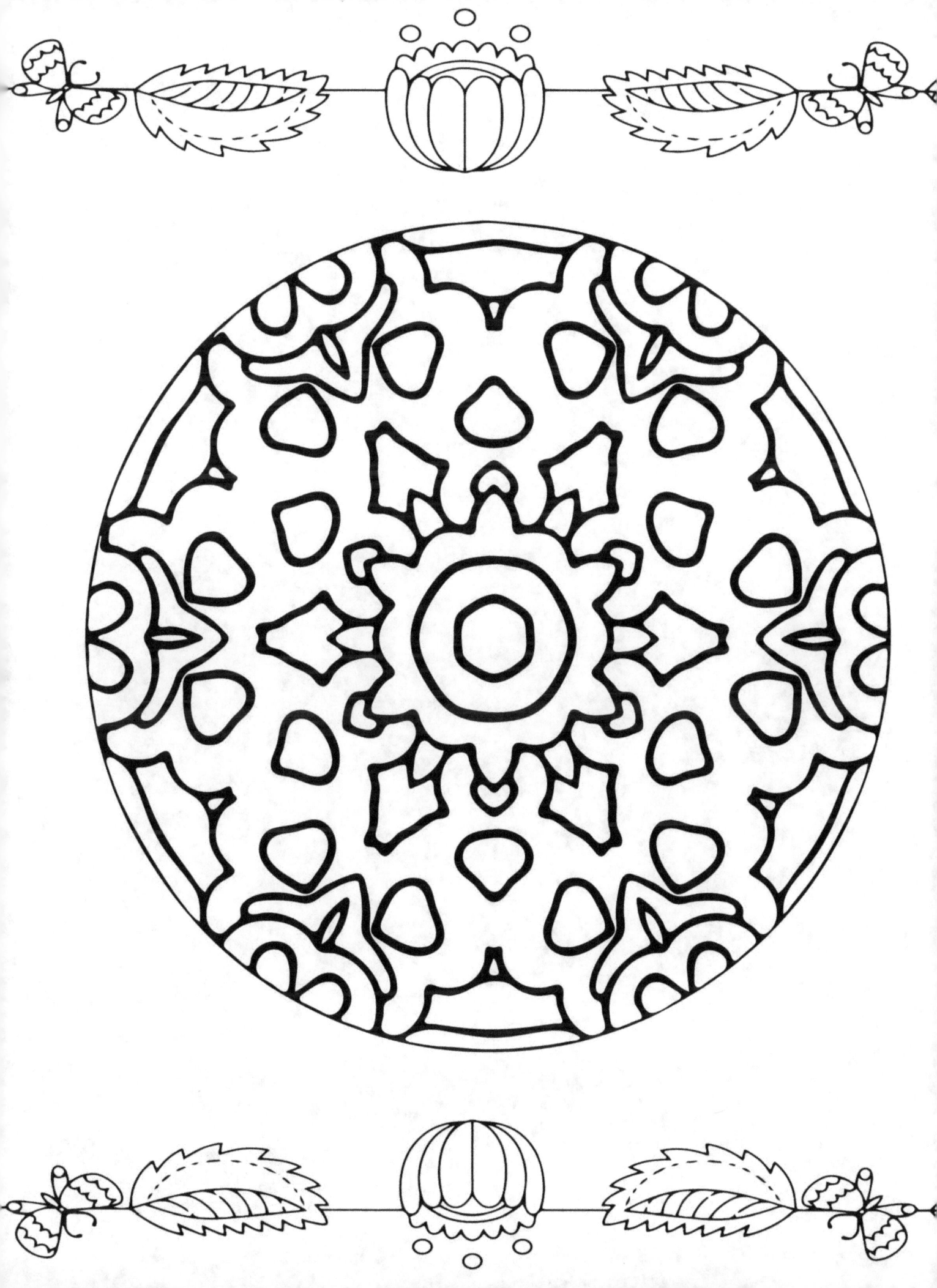

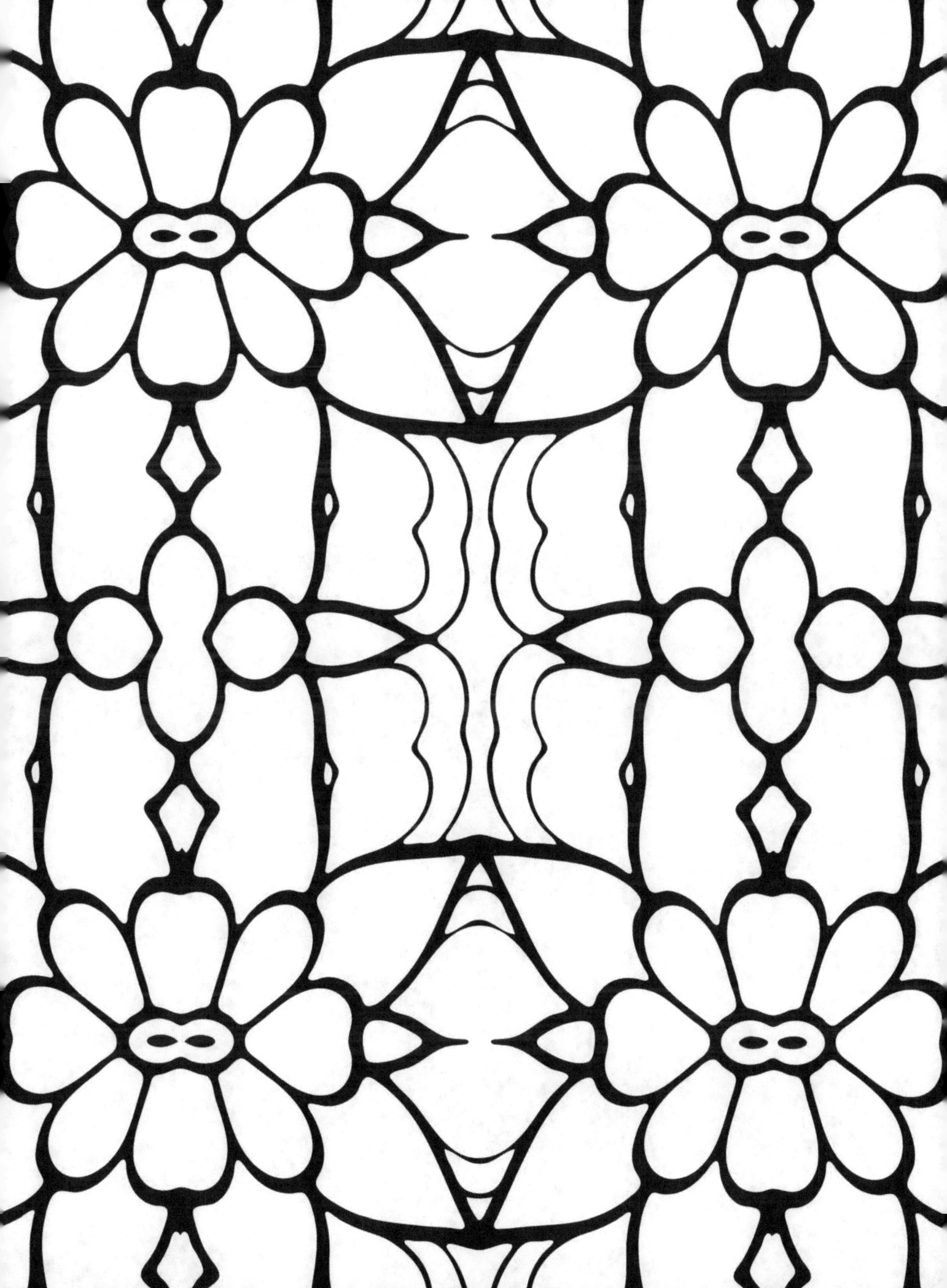

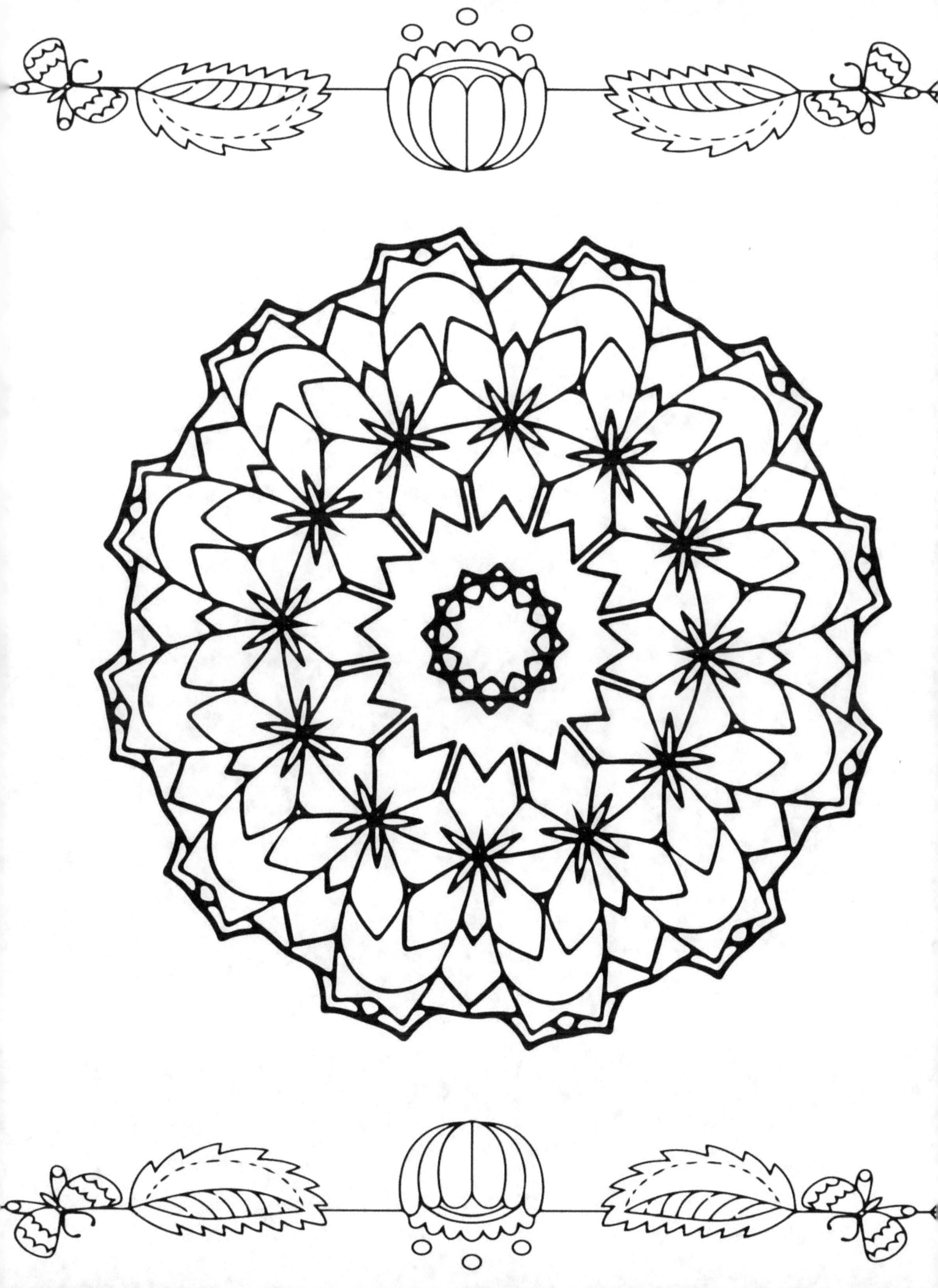

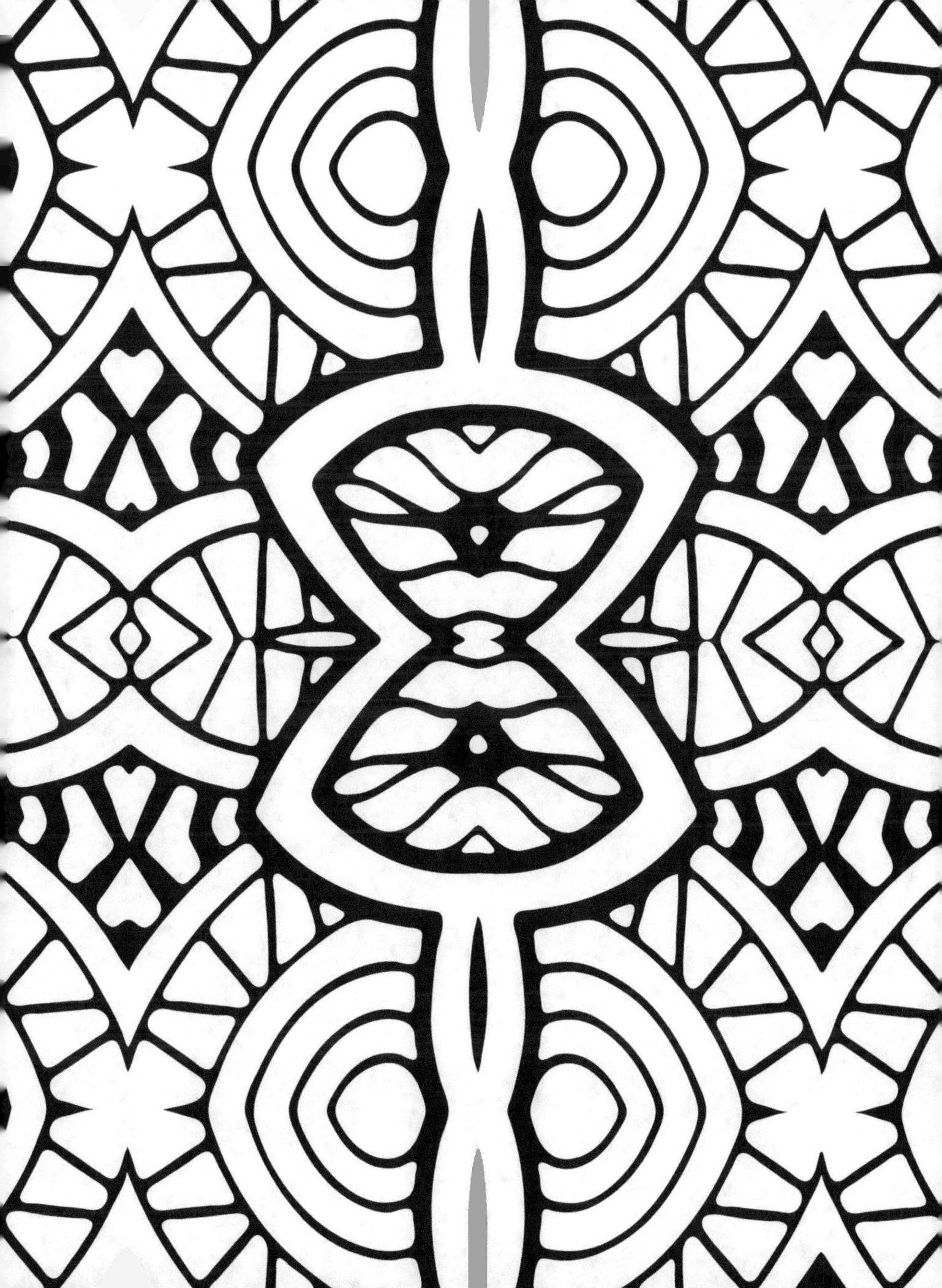

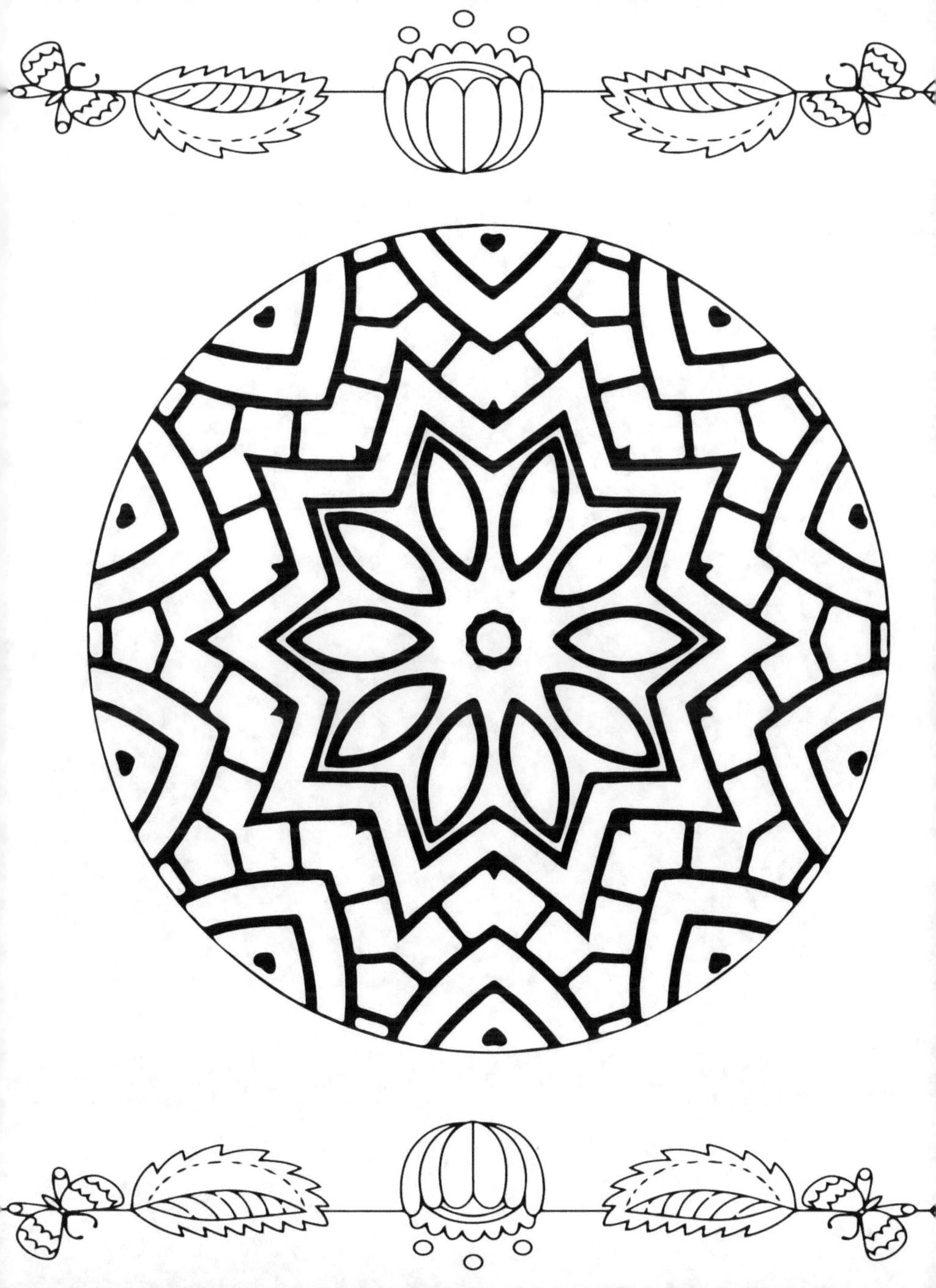

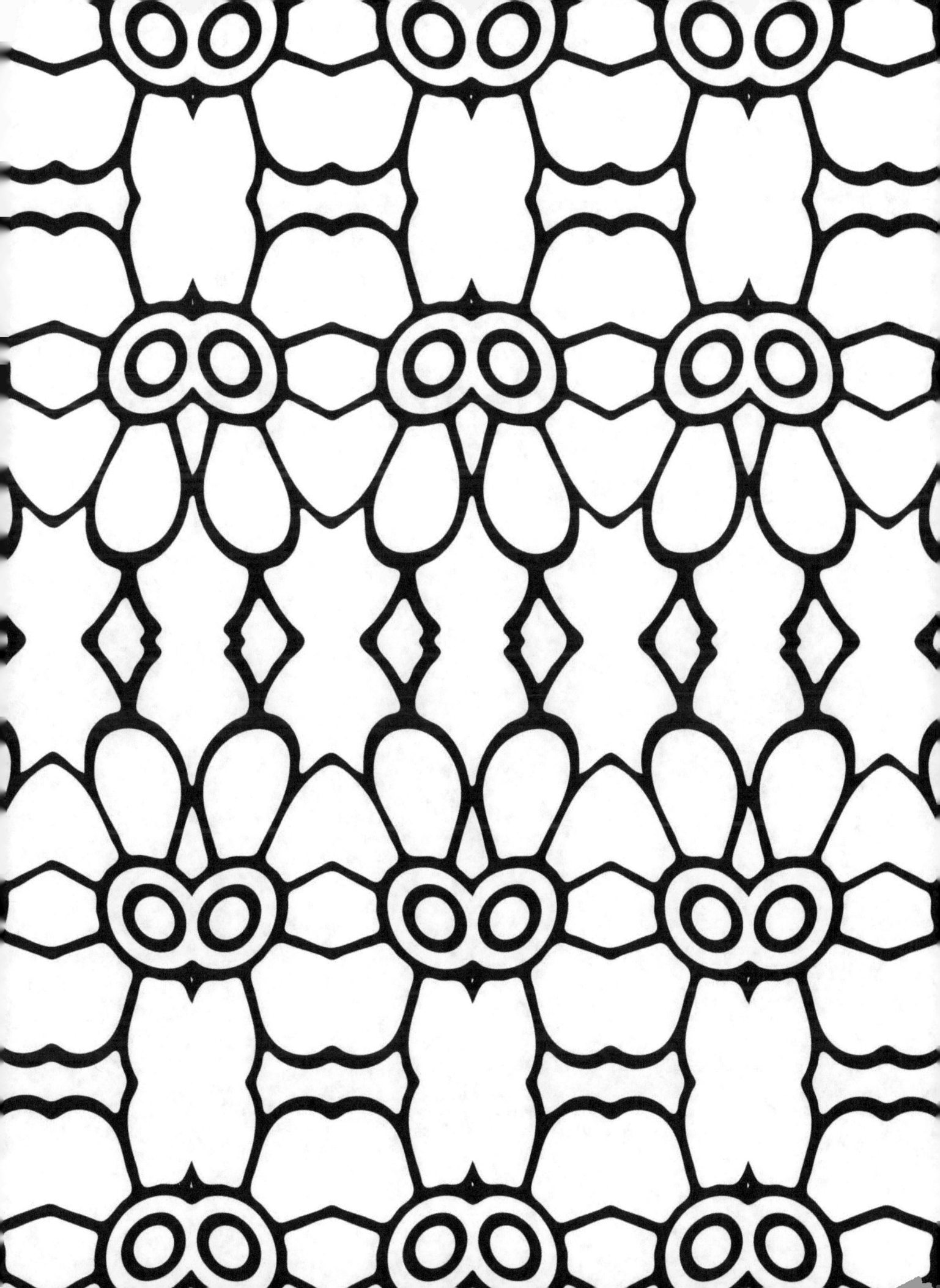

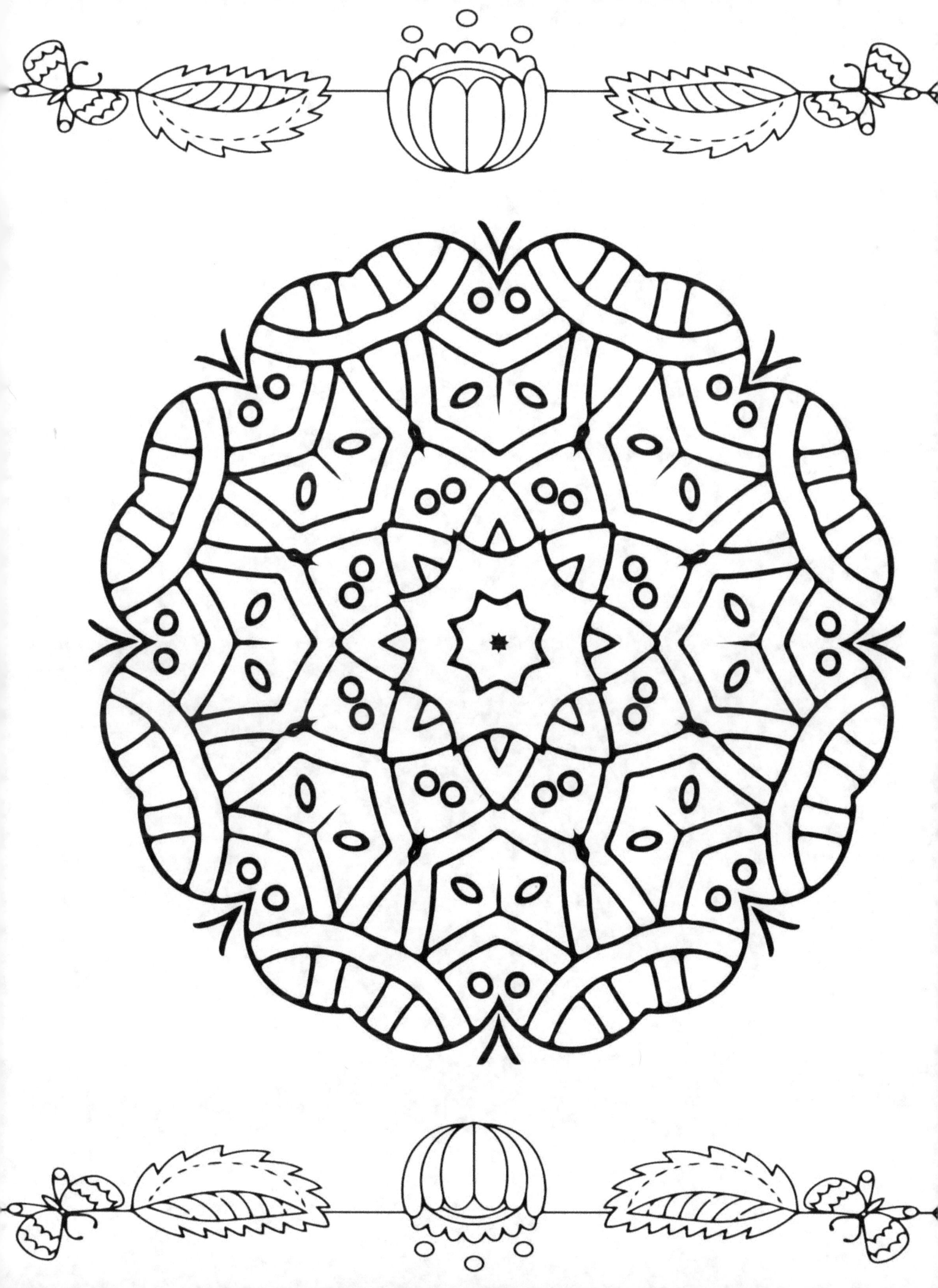

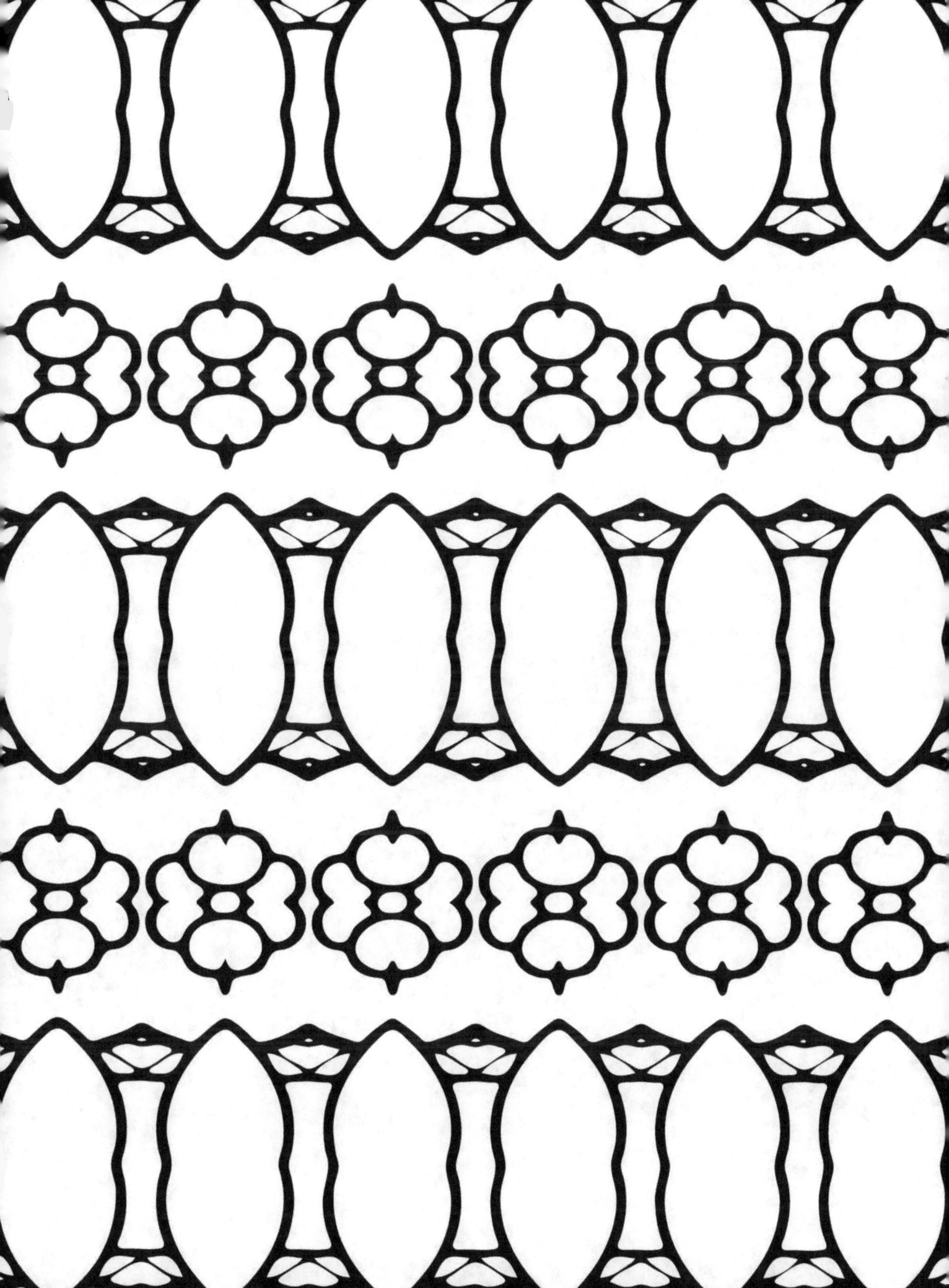

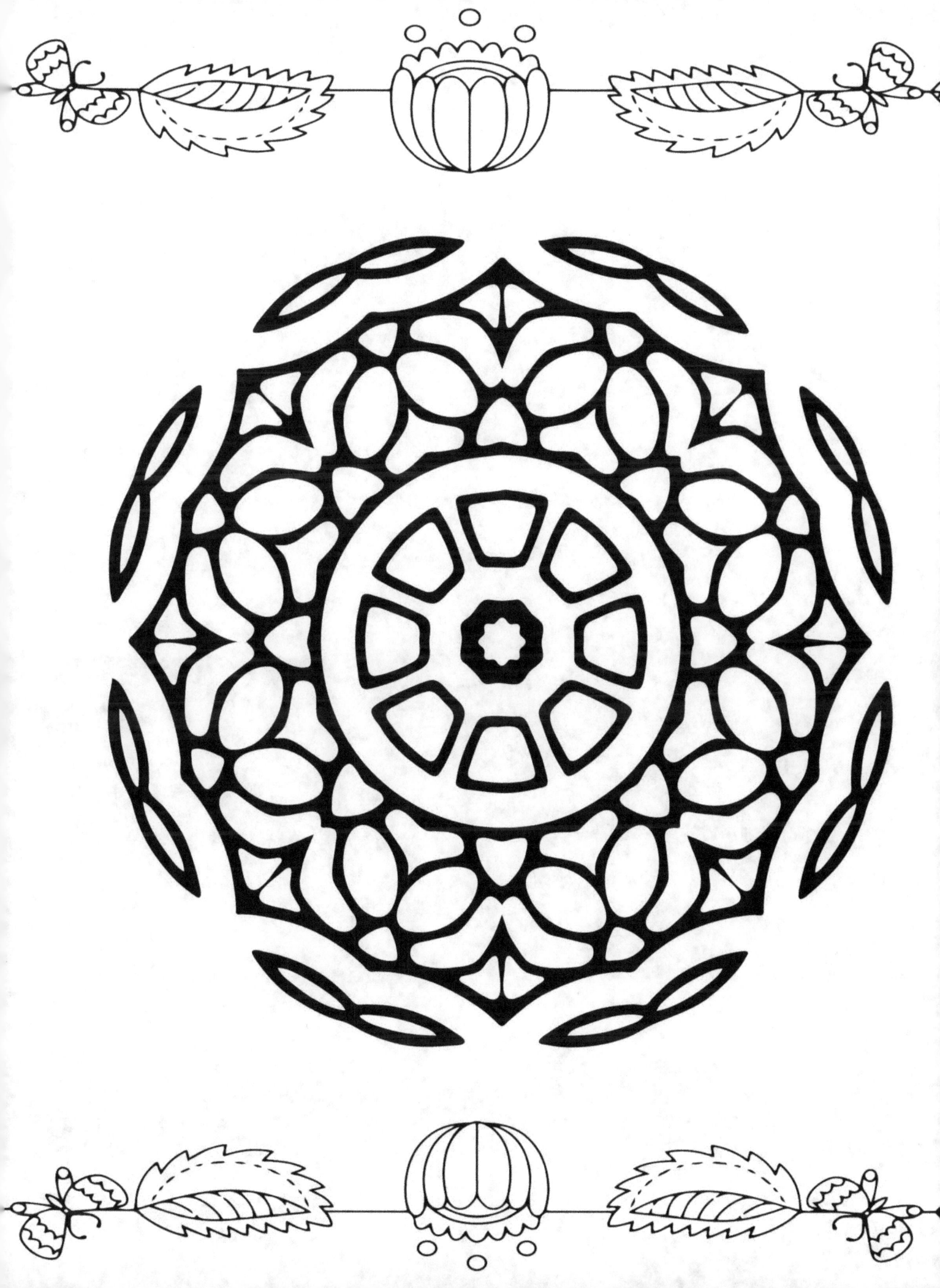

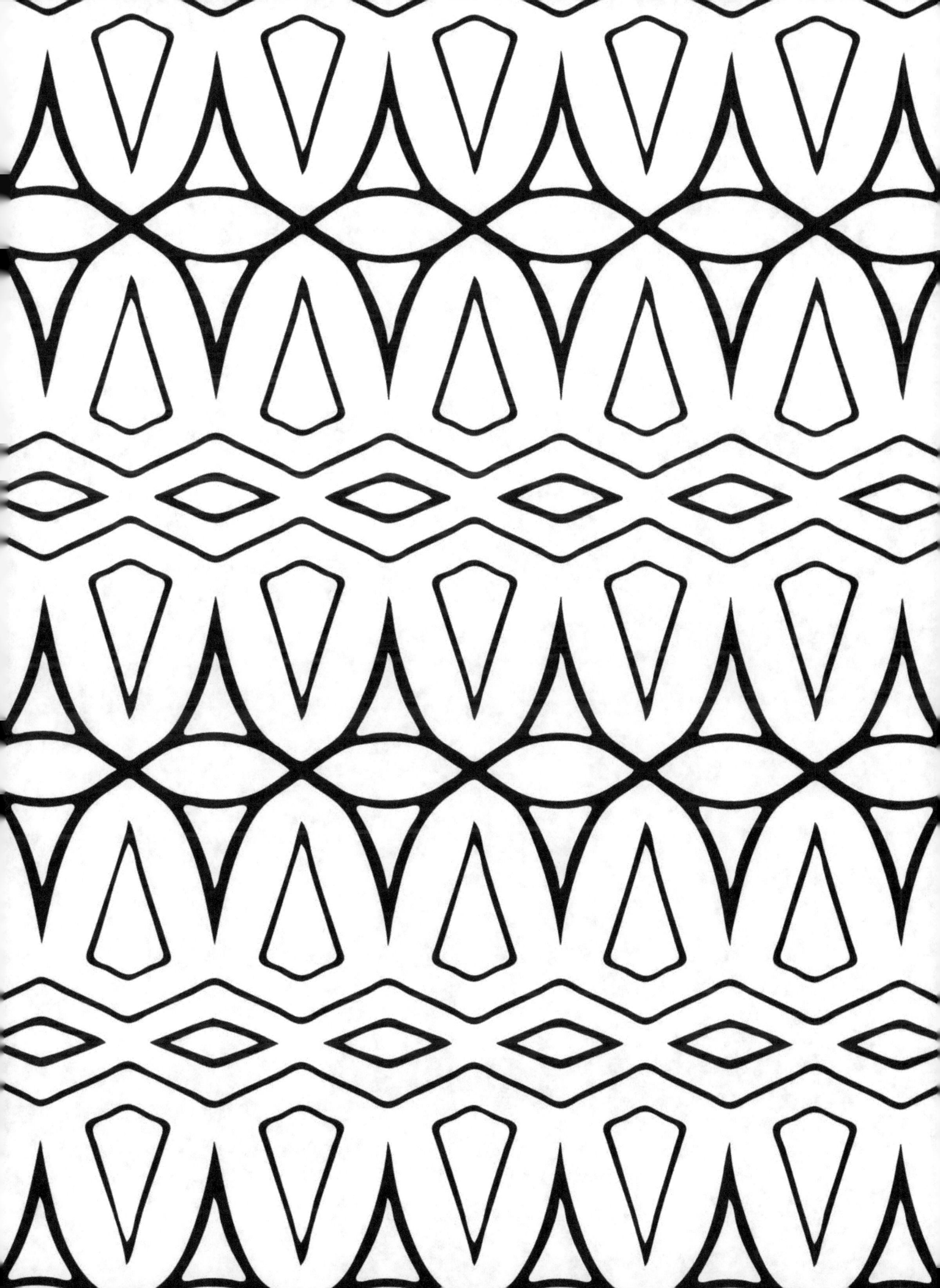

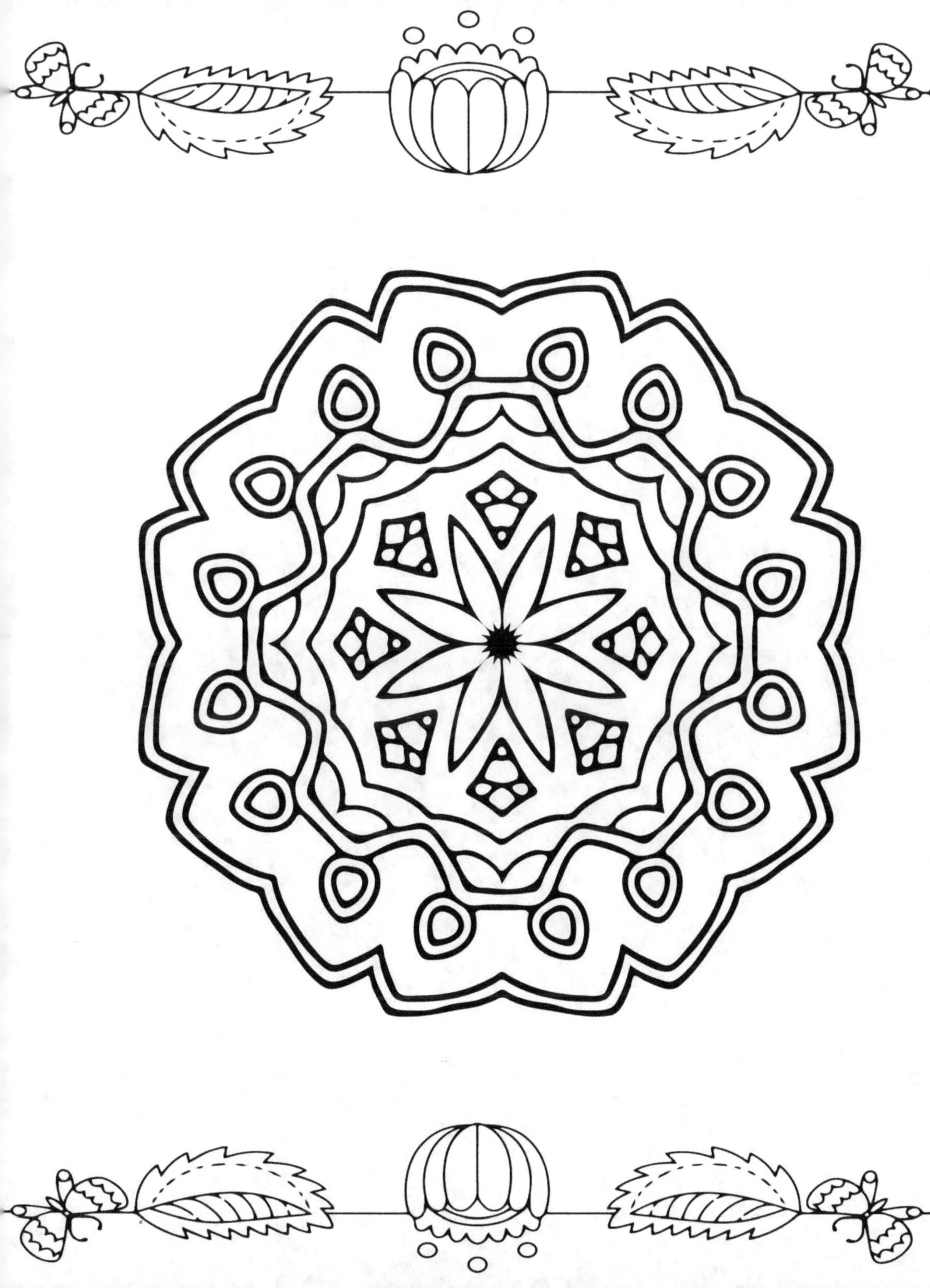

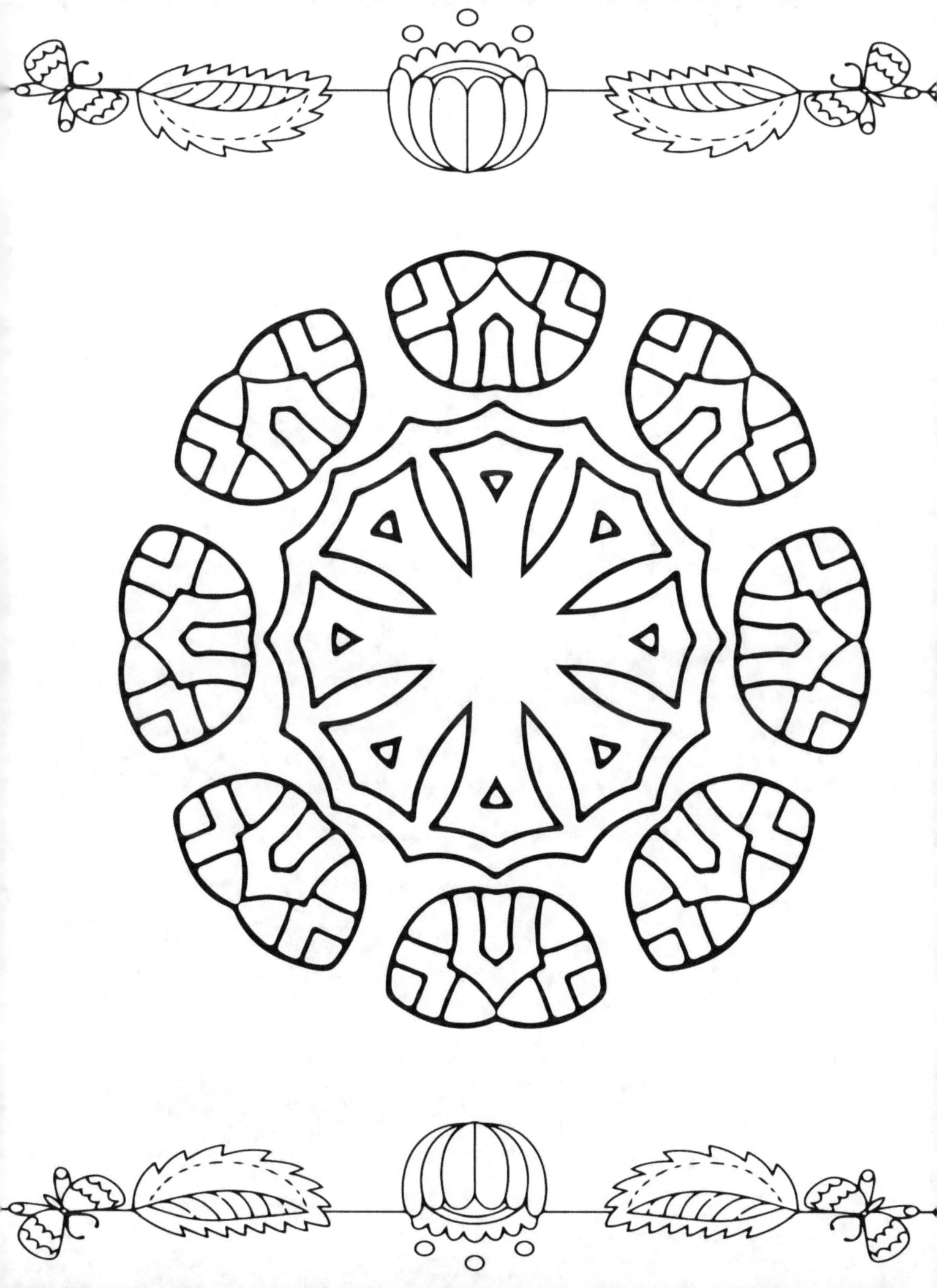

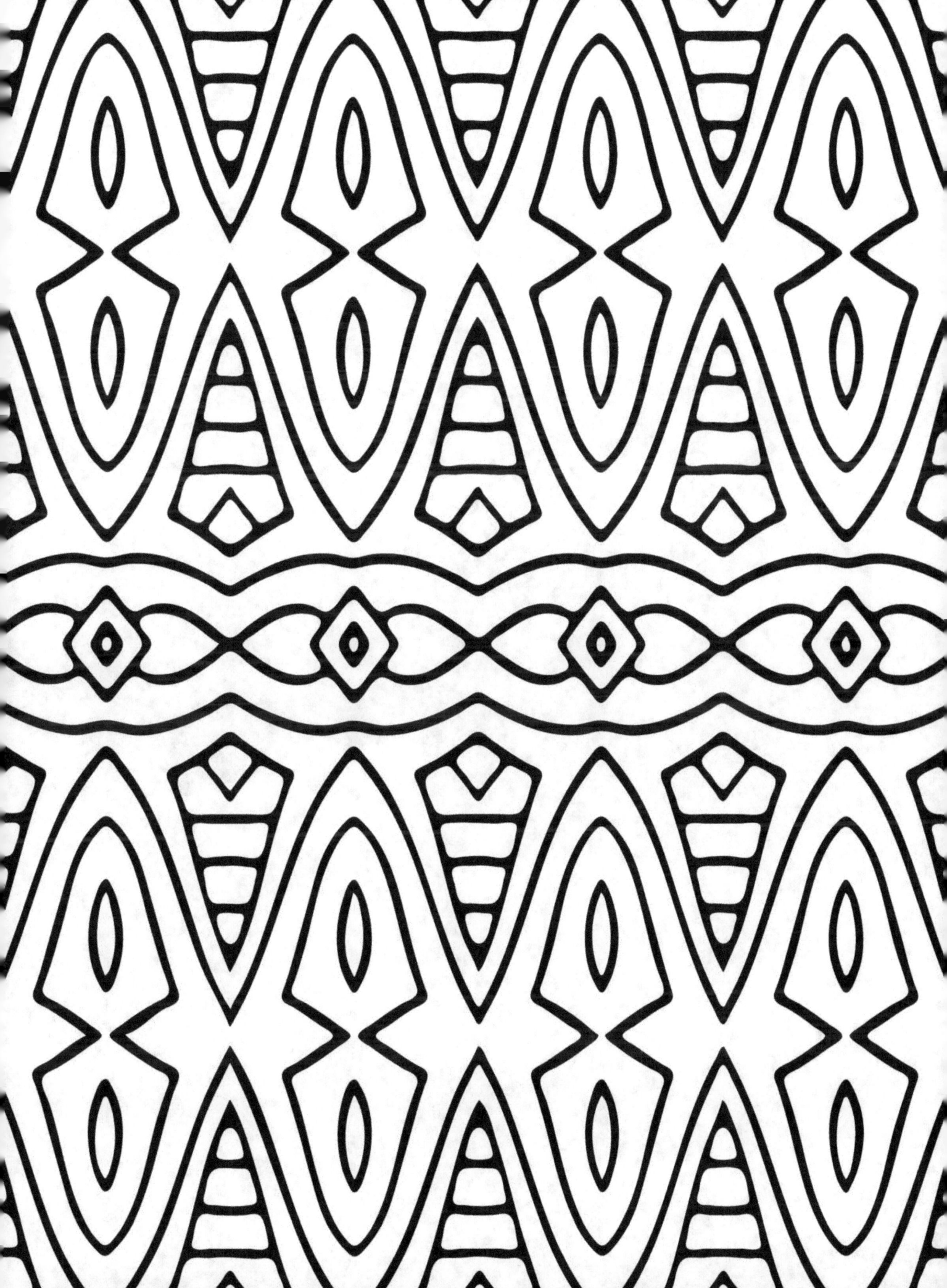

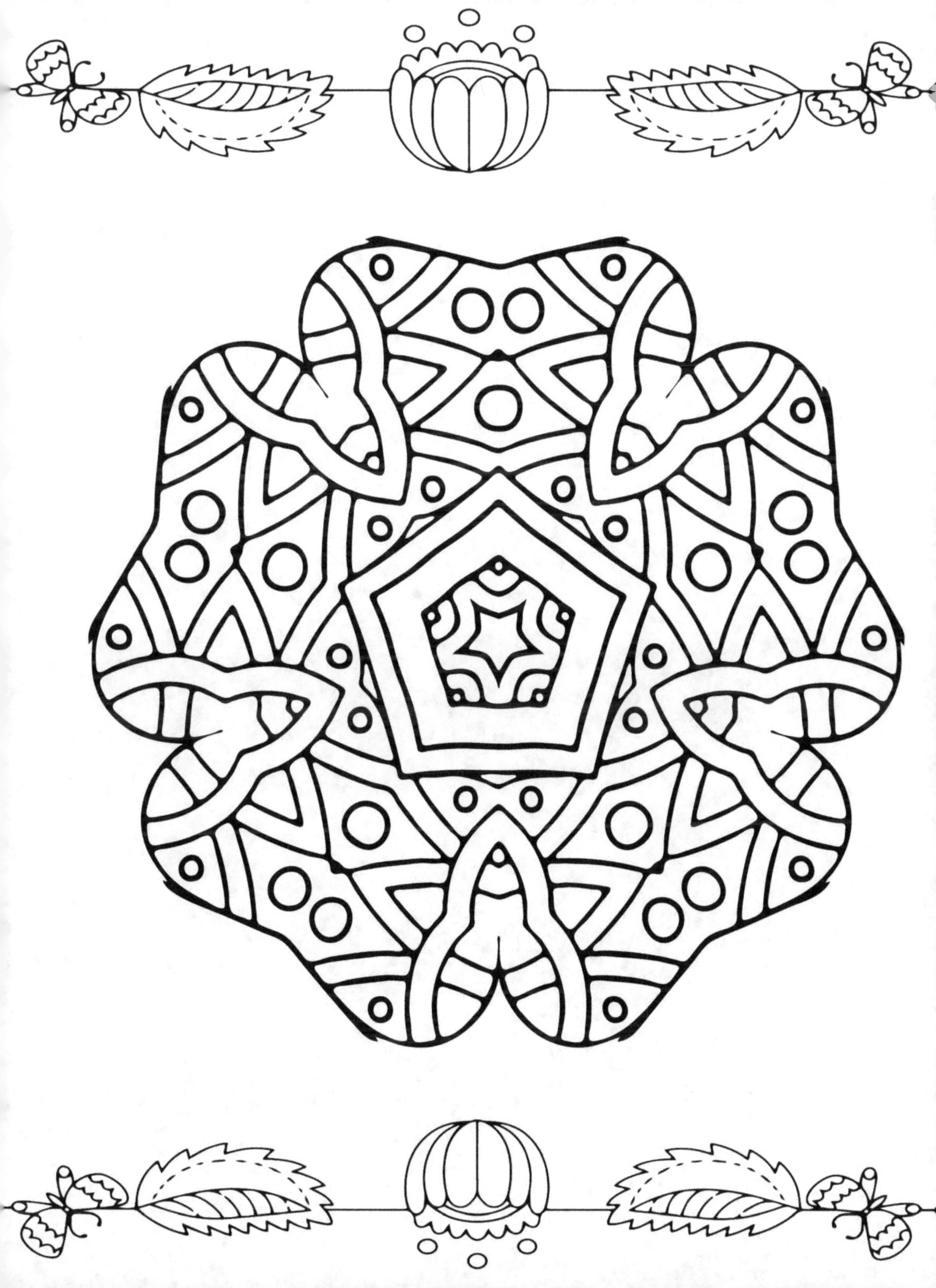

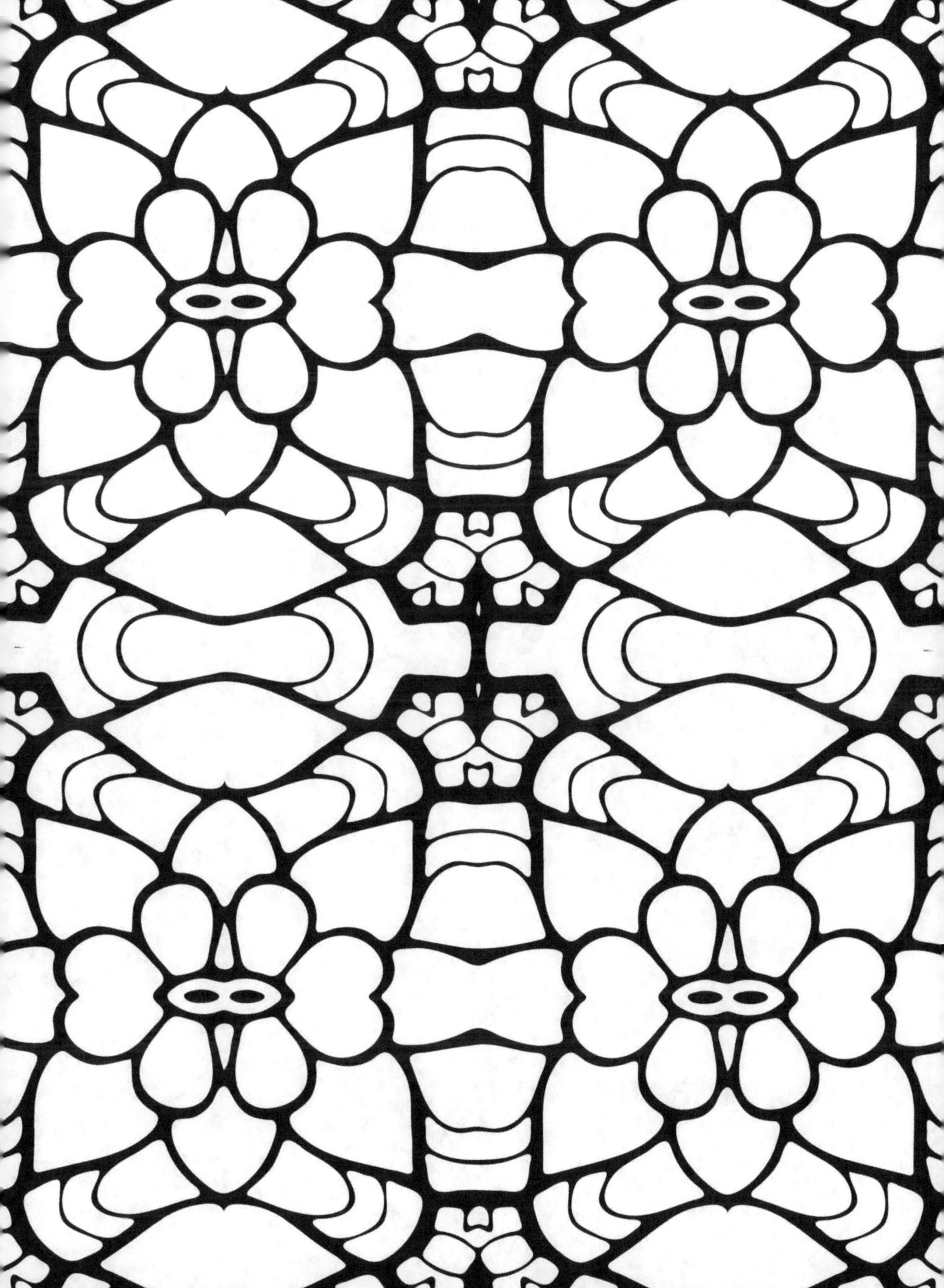

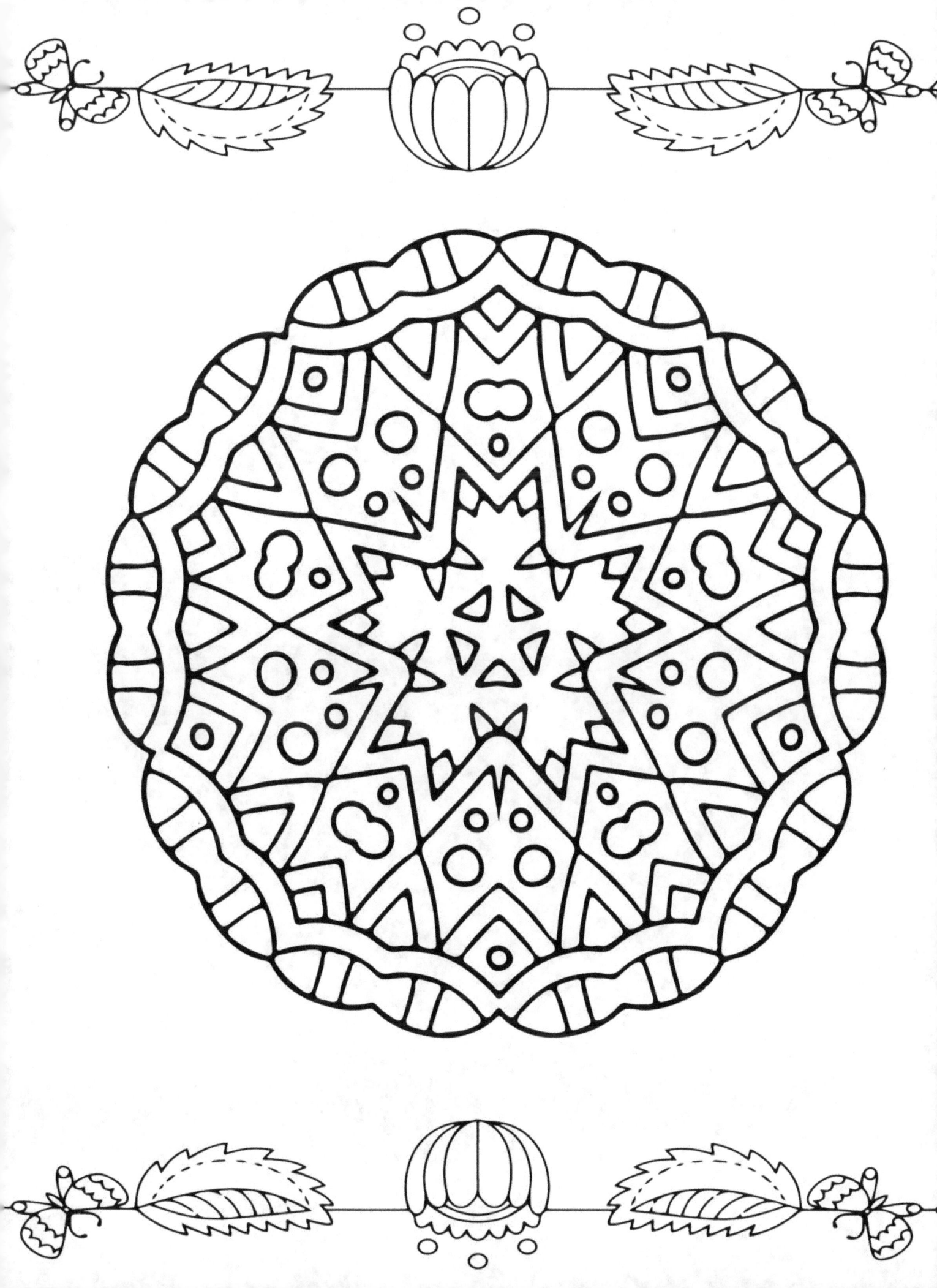

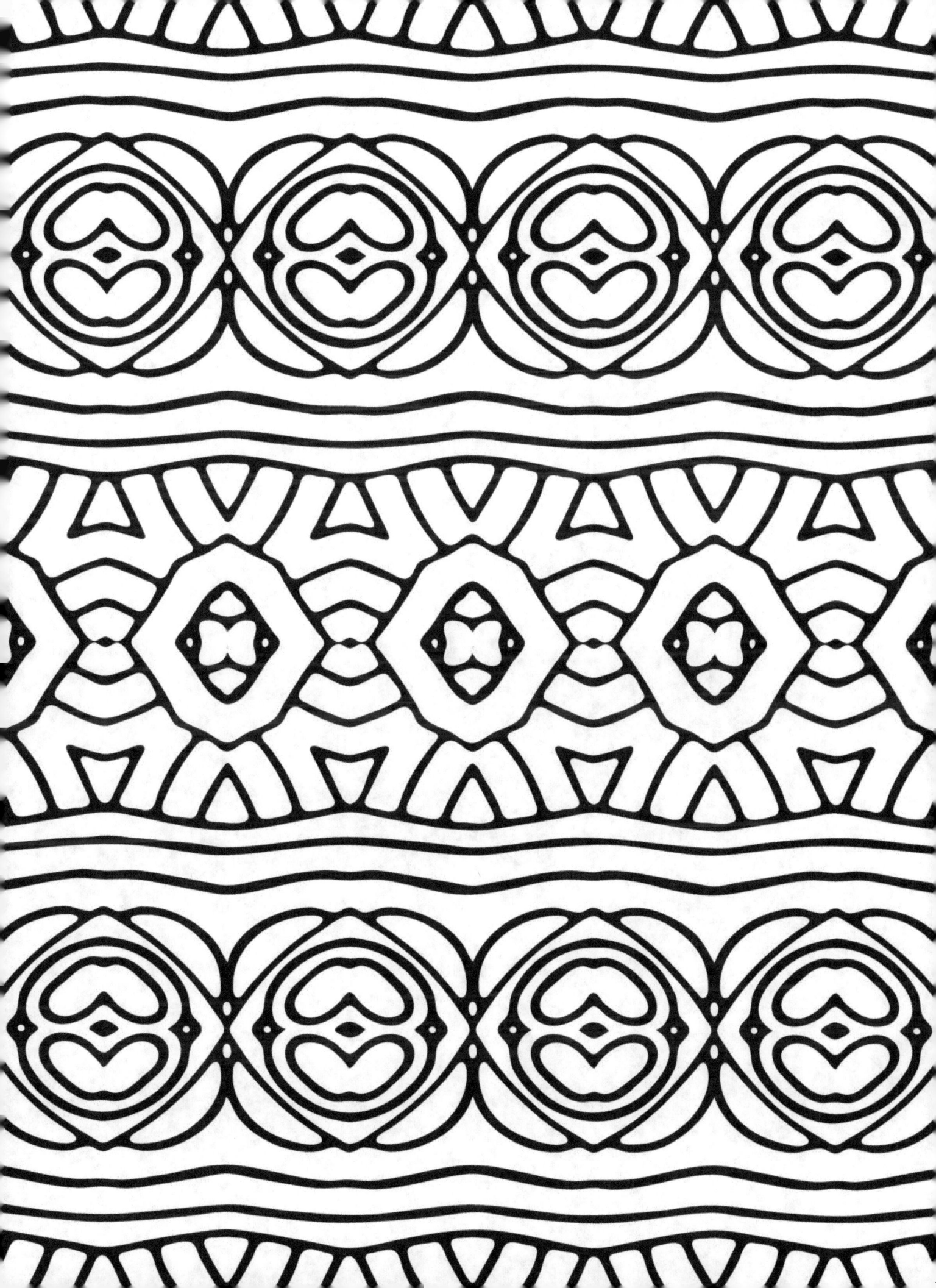

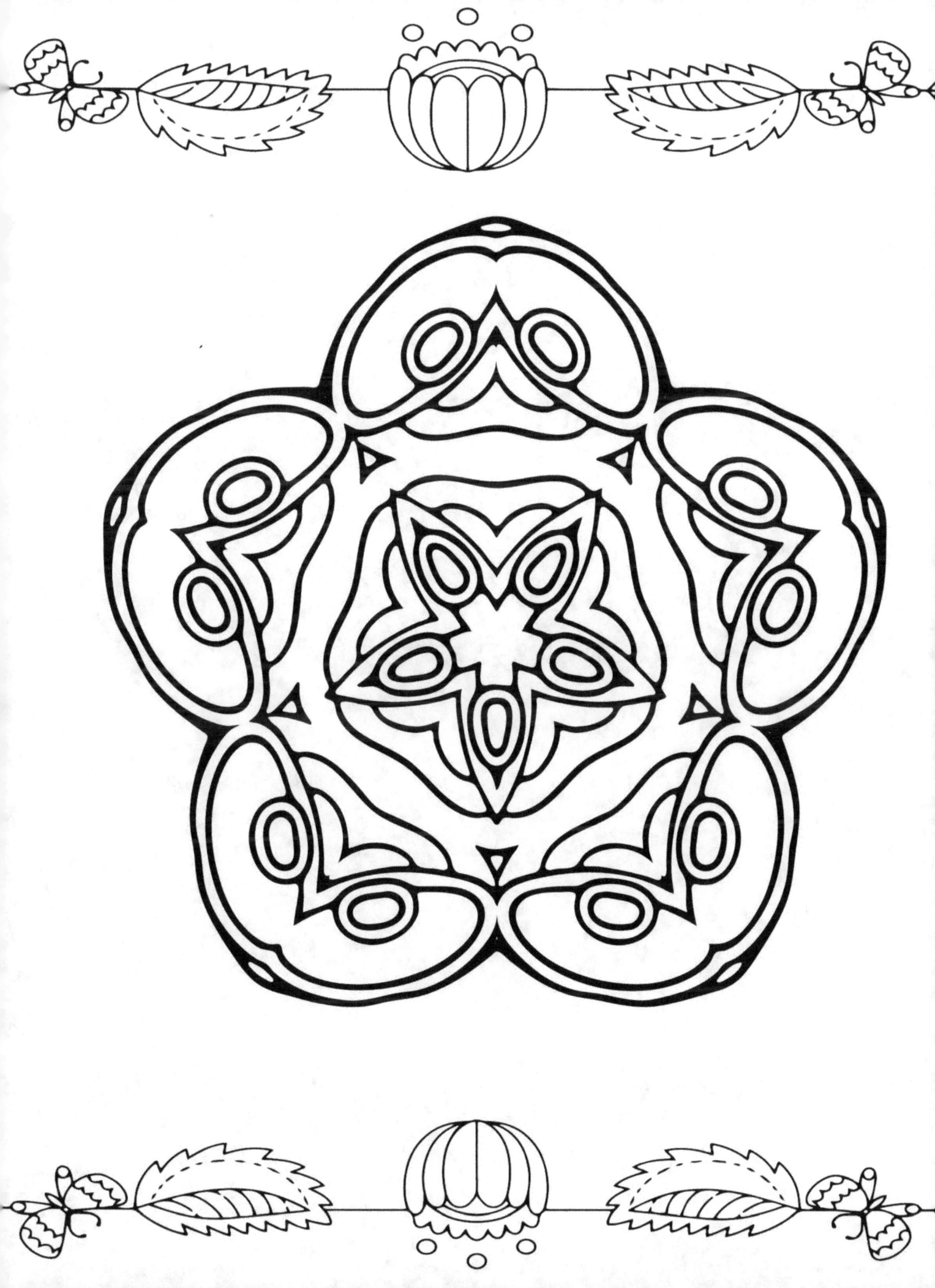

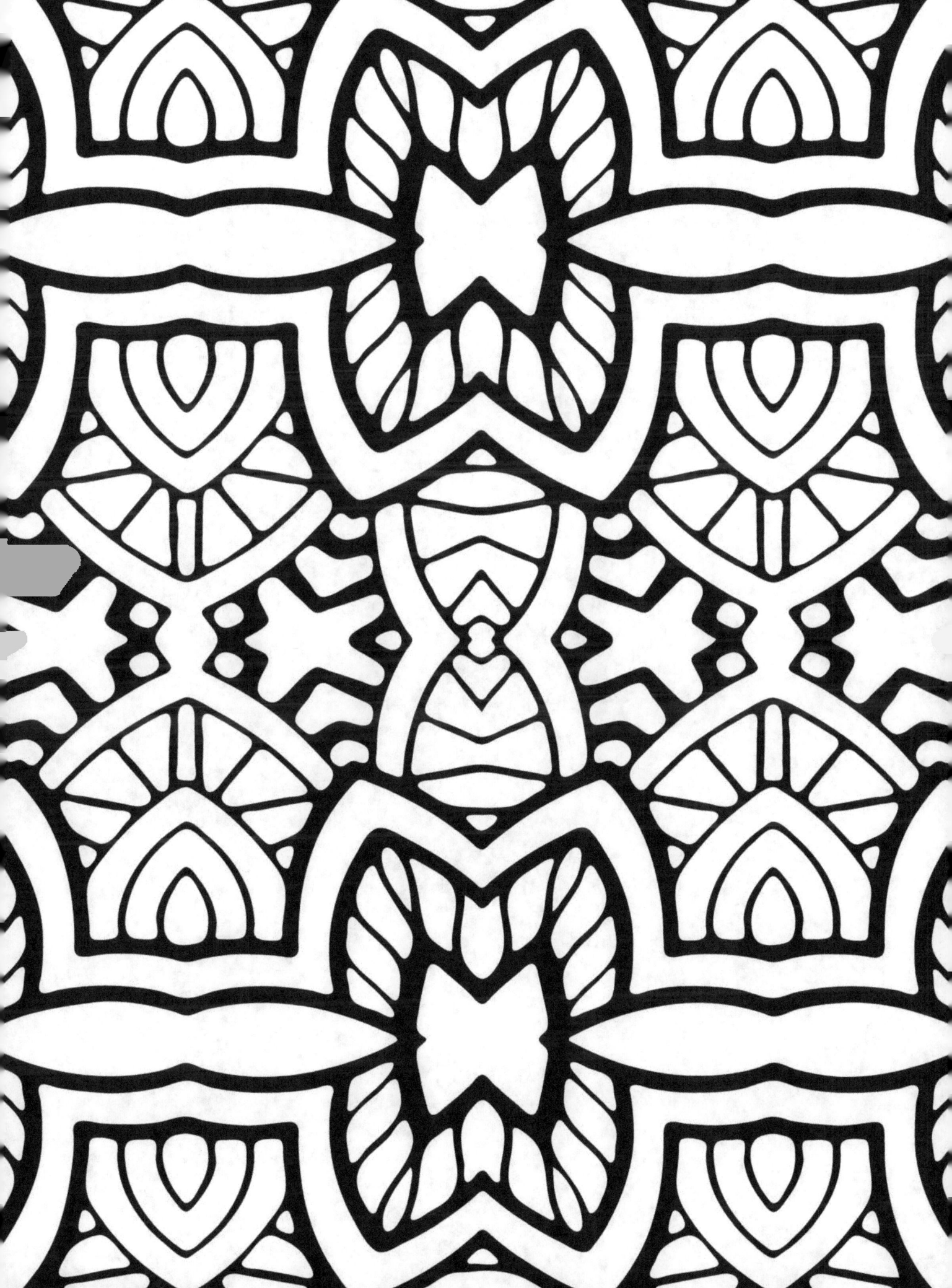

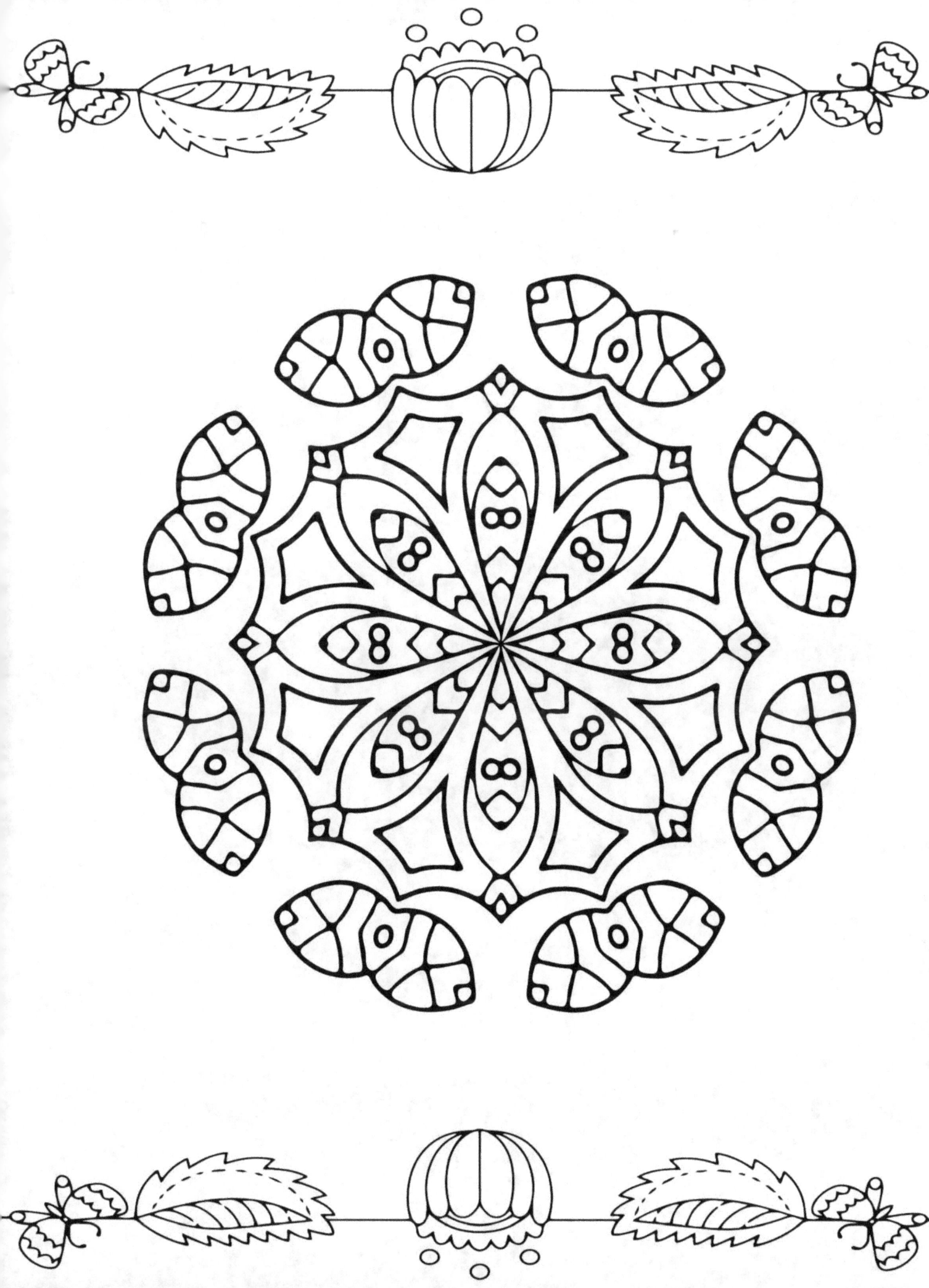

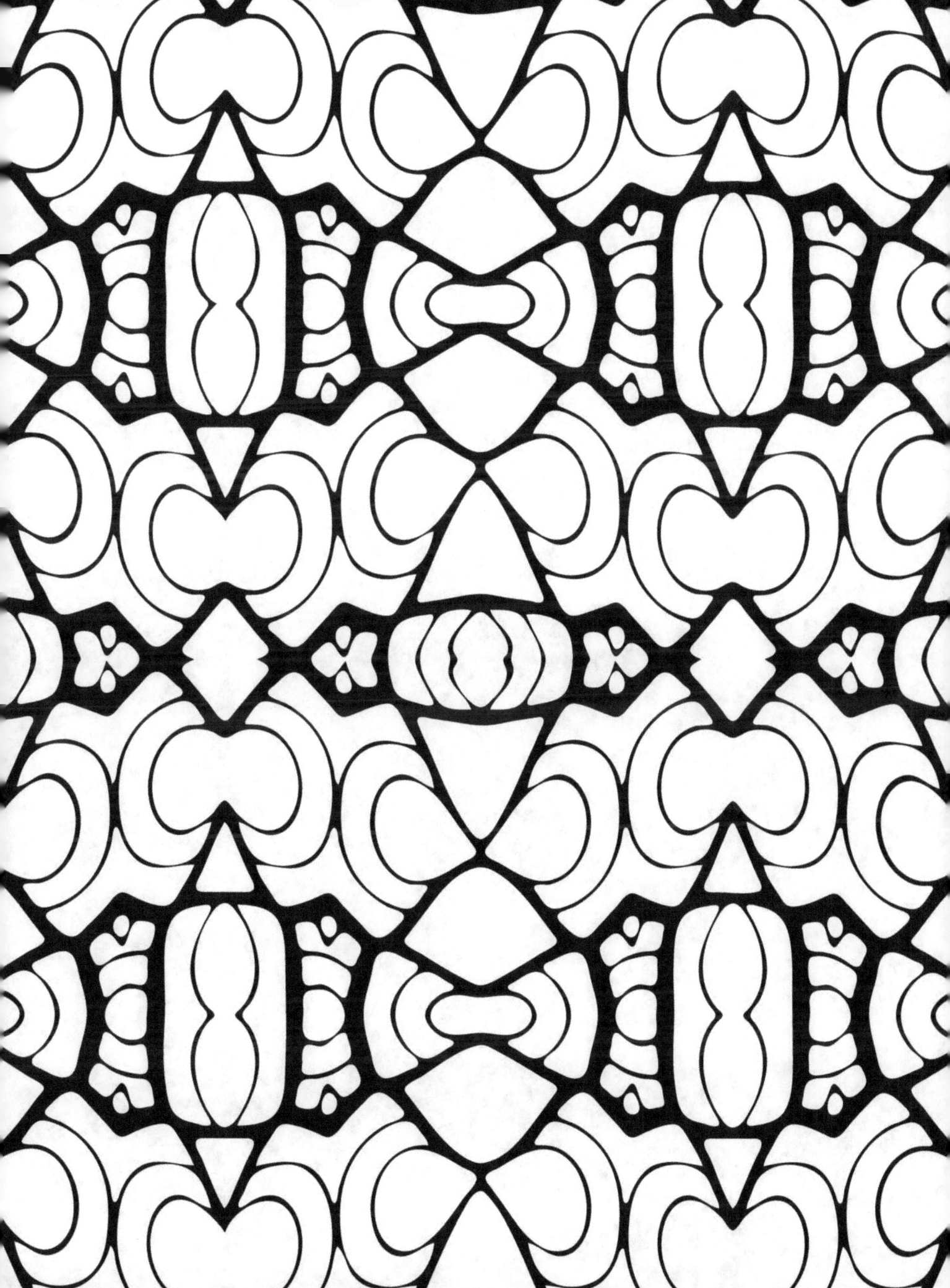

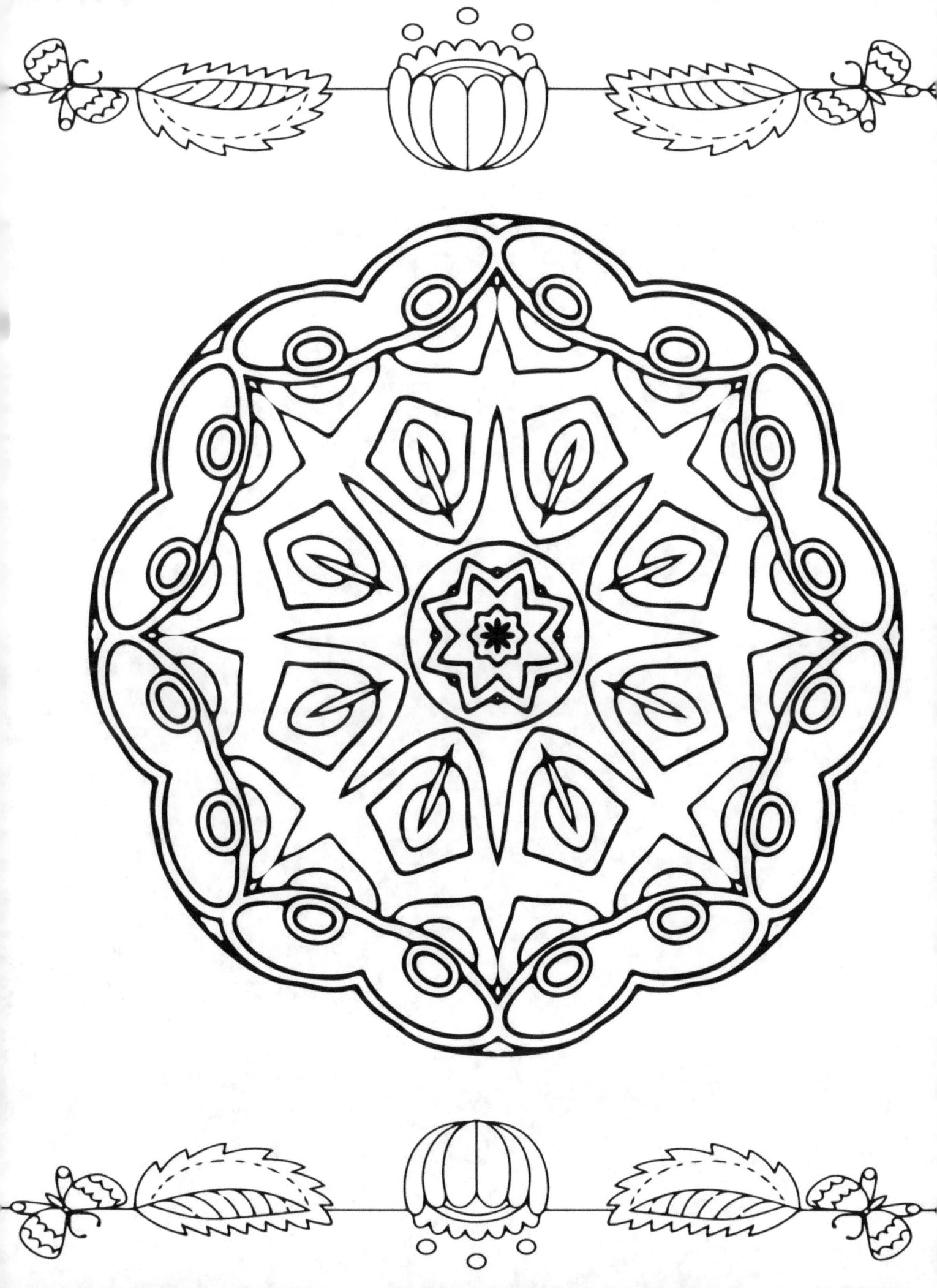

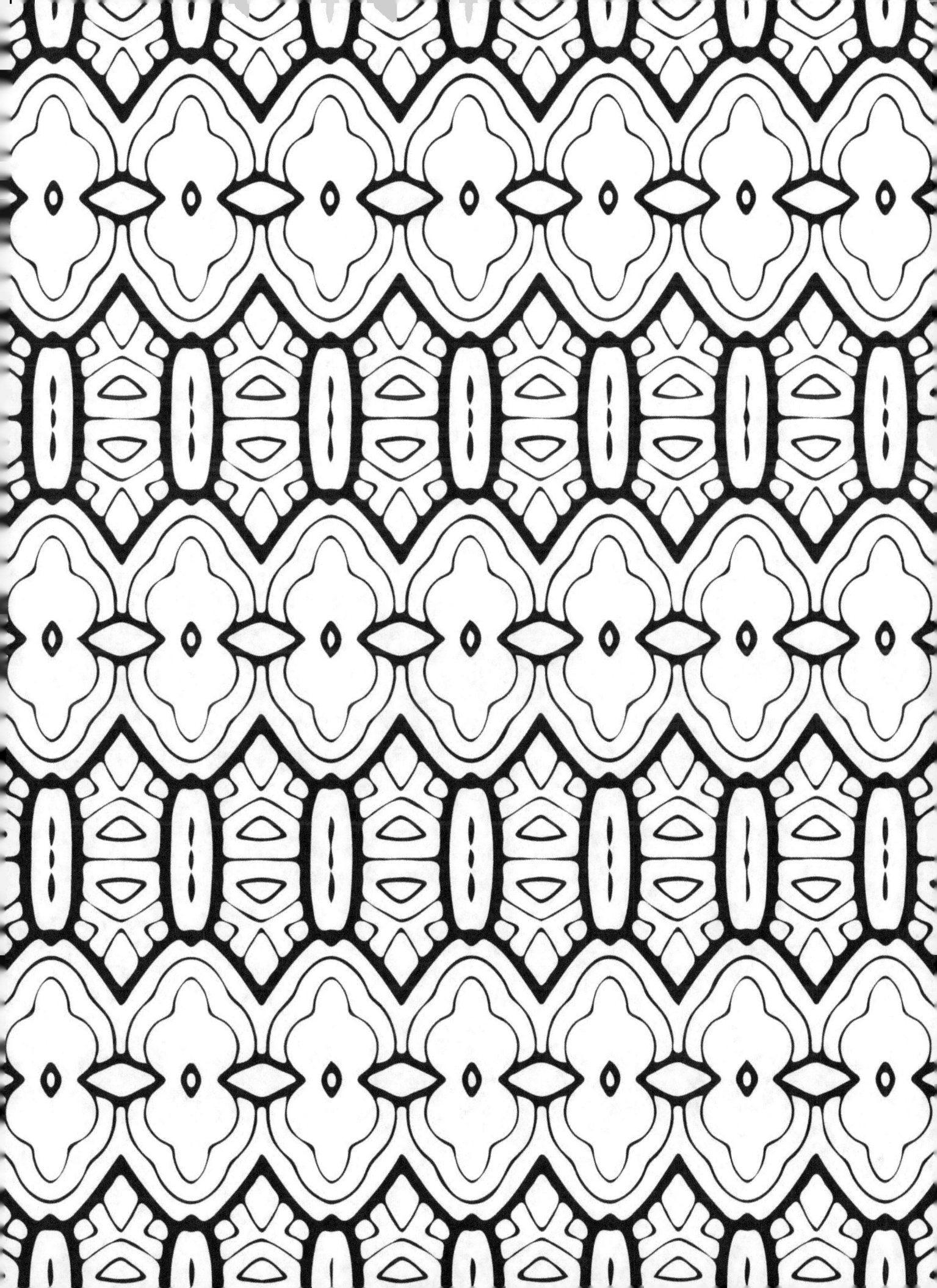

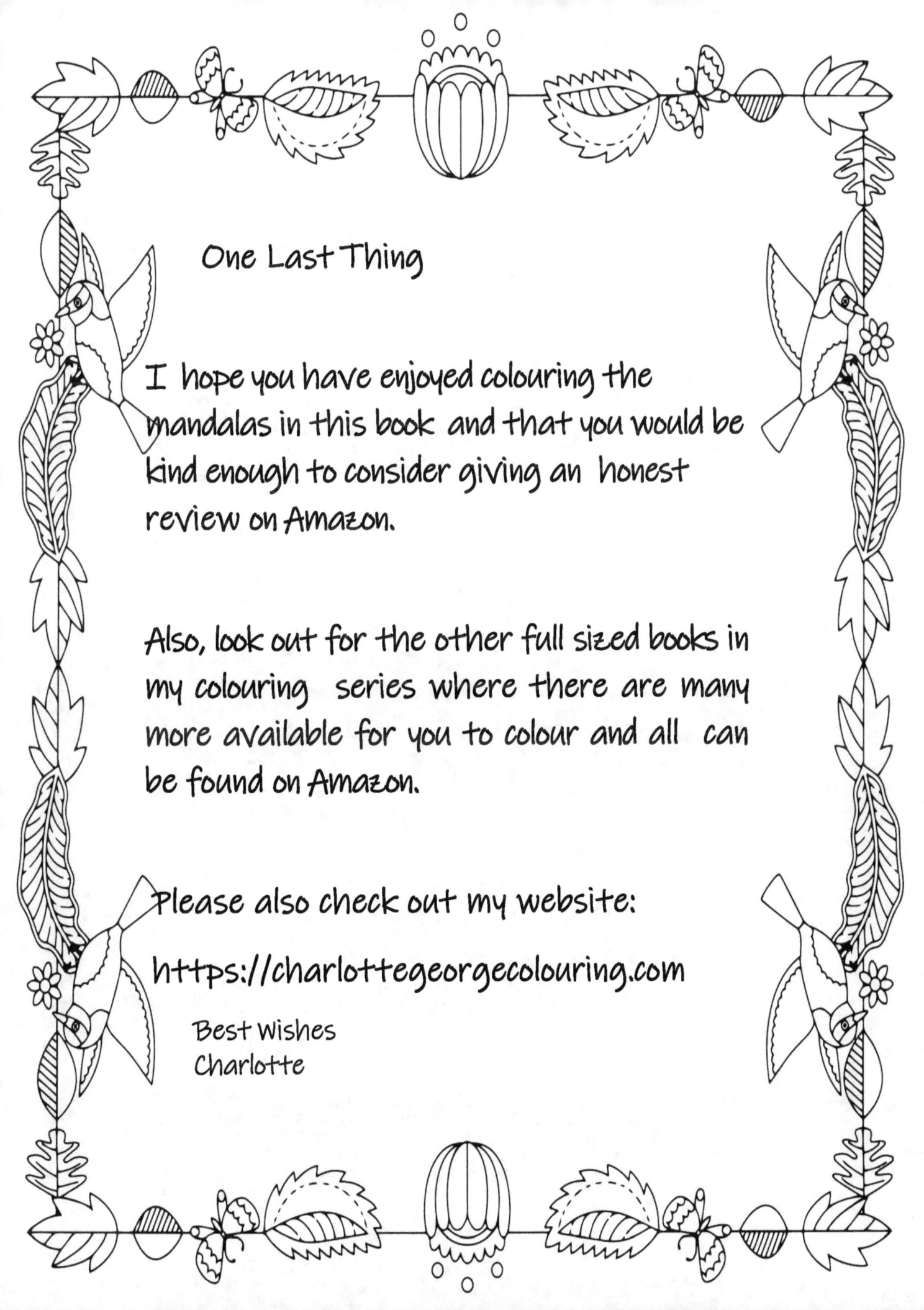

One Last Thing

I hope you have enjoyed colouring the mandalas in this book and that you would be kind enough to consider giving an honest review on Amazon.

Also, look out for the other full sized books in my colouring series where there are many more available for you to colour and all can be found on Amazon.

Please also check out my website:

https://charlottegeorgecolouring.com

Best Wishes
Charlotte